*The
Kids' Book
About
Single-Parent
Families*

The Kids' Book About Single-Parent Families

Kids for Everyone

Edited by

Paul Dolmetsch
Alexa Shih

A DOLPHIN BOOK
DOUBLEDAY & COMPANY, INC.
GARDEN CITY, NEW YORK
1985

Library of Congress Cataloging in Publication Data
I. Dolmetsch, Paul. II. Shih, Alexa
The kids' book about single parent families.

"A Dolphin book."
Summary: Children describe their experiences and problems living with a single
parent, including unmarried mothers, divorced parents, and parents whose spouses
have died.
1. Children of single parents—Juvenile literature. 2. Single parents—Juvenile
literature. 3. Family—Juvenile literature. [1. Single-parent family. 2. Family life]
II. Title.

HQ777.4.D65 1985   306.8'56   84-21156
ISBN 0-385-19279-7

Printed in the United States of America

First Edition

To everyone who has lived, does live, and will live in a single-parent family

Acknowledgments

We are most grateful to Eric Rofes, Helen Rees, and Lindy Hess who allayed our fears and guided us to the book's completion, and we also thank the Cleveland Dodge Foundation for its generosity. This book represents the effort of an entire community. We are particularly indebted to Martha Rudd, Anthony Krulikowski, and Thomas Curran, administrators of the Mount Anthony Junior and Senior High Schools, and to Michel Kimball, Director of the Child/Adult Department at United Counseling Service, for their enthusiastic support. A special thanks to Gisela Lehovec, the children's librarian at the Bennington Free Library, who helped us with our book reviews.

And finally, we also appreciate the countless children and adults who gave us their views of ongoing life in single-parent families. We want to thank others for their advice and encouragement during the two years that we labored over the content and technical details of publishing a book.

Alan Asher	Maureen Matthews
Scott Asher	Sandy Mausert
Robert Becker	Sally Mole
Marilyn Becker	Maryanne Nesbitt
Mary Becker	Greta Ouimette
Mary Ellen Breen	Eleanor Pulver
Sally Cahill	Charles Putney

Debi Cardillo   Brin Quell
John Chapin   Linda Remington
Marie Condon   Stephen Saltonstall
Matthew Daigneault   William Scott
Nicholas Delbanco   Lois Seenan
Meridale Dupree   Joseph Sourdiffe
James Henry   John Soward
Anna Horbert   Sally Sugarman
Marny Krause   Elizabeth Vigsnes
Gerrit Kouwenhoven   Elizabeth Winship
Thomas Jacobs   Margaret Winship
Ernest Lafontaine   Ginger Wood
Robert Lasher   Doris Zampini

Contents

Introduction

United Counseling Service began this project for the purpose of giving recognition to the richness of people's lives in single-parent families. The goal is to help make single-parent families stronger and more able environments in which to raise happy, healthy, and hopeful children.

As editors, we have both professional and personal reasons for wanting a book produced by children about growing up in single-parent families. In our work as a psychiatric social worker and a director of prevention programs for youth, we are faced with the changing needs of today's families. We are aware of more and more families becoming single-parent families. It is projected that half of all children below the age of eight will spend some portion of their lives in these families. Also true is that single-parent families are opting to remain so for longer periods of time.

Personally, each of us grew up in a single-parent family. Our experiences make us sensitive to the needs of children who live in single-parent families. Though our family situations were each quite different, we are cognizant of predictable areas of strength and vulnerability in these children.

There is no evidence to suggest that single-parent families are inherently good or bad. All require, because of the nature of their beginnings, adjustments by parents and kids. We think that there is much more that can be done by parents, kids, school personnel, mental health professionals, lawyers, judges, and employers to help single-parent families. Our society is adapting, but we still see the need for more accurate, appealing information. We think that this book will help people to have a clearer understanding of life for kids in single-parent families.

Our idea to gather a group of teenagers to write this book grew out of the work of Eric Rofes and the kids from the Fayerweather Street School in Cambridge, Massachusetts. Their book, *The Kids' Book of Divorce*, demonstrates that youth, with direction, can communicate with other children and adults in a way that is fresh, moving, and relevant.

We began the project with a mixture of excitement and fear. The path to the final manuscript was not always clear, and we worried each step of the way. Would kids volunteer for the project? Would parents allow them to discuss their lives? Would the school system interrupt carefully arranged schedules so that kids could work together in a comfortable and natural setting? Even if all those problems were solved, would we be able to produce a work with the kids that was publishable material? We were haunted by these questions from the outset to the completion of the manuscript.

We owe what we can happily say our success to the unqualified support of our entire community. The Executive Director of United Counseling Service, Carole O'Neal, backed the project with determined vision when it was nothing more than one more good idea. The Superintendent of the Southwest Vermont Supervisory Union, George Sleeman, and staff of the school system opened their doors to us and never closed them. The staff of United Counseling Service stayed interested in what we were doing and took care of our every need. The continual cooperation and support of friends, colleagues, and professionals in the community kept our spirits up when we were most weary. And, of course, without the incredible patience of our own families who had to struggle with our preoccupation, this project never would have been completed. Most importantly, the student-authors and their parents gave us their implicit and explicit trust, a most precious gift.

We thought that our idea to have a diverse group of children write a book about growing up in single-parent families would contribute to the well-being of the community. We now believe that there are far-reaching benefits for the student-authors, for future mental health and educational program planners, and for all those who share an interest in the quality of life in single-parent families.

Our most exciting discovery from the time that we spent with the group of young authors is the usefulness of having adolescents write and publish on topics of social importance. We learned from the student-authors, not only about the particulars of each of their lives but also about the ethics, values, and capabilities of adolescents in general. As a result, we have developed a great respect for kids' creativity in managing a continually changing world.

We realized that the ability to be a good social observer is not necessarily tied to academic performance. Each member of the group had his or her own way of contributing. Often kids who were not considered good students would have insightful and eloquent understandings of family life.

Our greatest pleasure from this project was the dedication and commitment of the student-authors. They astounded us. For nearly eighteen months, through two long Vermont winters and one short Vermont summer, the group met, discussed, argued, laughed, interviewed, wrote, and edited. The tenacity of the kids confounded many notions about the shortness of the adolescent attention span. Each member had his or her own reasons for sticking with the project. We believe that their efforts were fueled by having their words and thoughts respected.

Our experience suggests models for innovative productive roles for adolescents in communities. We have to admit that we can no longer protect our children from all the forces of life which hamper a carefree childhood. There was a time in our society when adolescents were a more integral part of community life. They were needed in their families for economic survival. This is no longer true. For the most part, kids are required by our economic system to be consumers of goods and services and not contributors. As a result, adult and adolescent worlds are becoming increasingly isolated from each other.

We need to realize that kids cannot avoid the fears of the threat of nuclear war, terrorism, violence, economic problems, death, and divorce. Kids naturally work to manage these fears in order to keep them from interrupting their growth and happiness. Because of the distance between adults and adolescents, kids often reach certain determinations on their own or with peers. We believe that it is mutually beneficial for adolescents to get guidance and encouragement from adults.

We have observed that the group writing and publication process is a way of connecting the adult and the adolescent worlds. It gives kids a valued and productive role in a community. We are confident that on reading the kids' work anyone will recognize responsible, vital, and sensitive messages. Using this process, adults can tap and develop adolescents' creativity and productivity in any setting. It is a powerful tool in building adolescent self-confidence, self-understanding, and pride.

Our hope is that readers enjoy this book. One parent of a girl we interviewed said to us: "Almost never do we as parents get to know what is really on the minds of our children. I think it will be a real gift to us." So do we.

Authors

Elizabeth Albrycht

Darcey Baker

Julie Bird

Michelle Burrington

Norman Caraman

Tina Carey

Melissa Cone

Margae Diamond

Scott Eiser

Thomas Haley, III

Naomi Hamburg

Julie Haynes

Derek Hurley

Laura Jordan

Sheri Mulready

Stephen Peters

Jennifer Rancourt

Amyee Robinson

Faith Tudor

Noel Young

About Writing This Book

We got together when Paul and Alexa came to our English classes and asked who would be interested in writing a book about living in single-parent families. We all (if we were interested) had to get permission from our parents if they wanted us to be involved. After a few days, we were all interviewed by Paul and Alexa. They were really nice and seemed interested in us. There were ninety kids who wanted to write the book.

We met two days a week in school and talked about a lot of things. First, we just sat down and thought about everything that would be important to put in the book. Then we decided on the major issues and came up with the main outline. After that, we took each topic separately. We talked about it, wrote about it, and interviewed kids as well as adults.

We all learned so much by listening to each other. Of course, there were times when it was boring, and things just wouldn't "go." Sometimes we would fight and often we would laugh. And what that means is that we've become a sort of family. In the beginning, we talked about the definition of a family, and we decided that it doesn't have to be a mom, a dad, kids, and a dog. It can be just a group of people who care for each other. That's us!

None of us knew it took so much to write a book. We have all learned, as Tom said, "to answer *lots* of questions," to work in a group to get things done and, as Michelle said, "done right." From our group experience, we have learned to better cope with our own ways of lives and to understand other people's.

Each of us got something personal out of working on the book. These are some of our thoughts:

Stephen said, "I think I am stronger in decision-making now and more likely to stick to what I say. Also, I learned not to blame everything that happens in my family on me."

Tina said, "It helped me to gain a new perspective on life, and I'm more confident about who I am and what I do."

Darcey said, "I have learned that there are a lot of kids like me. I am also better at coping without a father."

Amyee said, "I'm now able to talk about my feelings and not hold them in."

Norman said, "I feel like I really know the subject."

Noel said, "I think I am more aware and realistic about my feelings."

Elizabeth said, "I am more mature, I think I handle stress better and *disappointment*. I have learned that you have to be strong but pliable. If you don't bend, you will break."

Julie B. said, "This book has been one of the better things that have happened to me. I feel good about my family and on top of that it was fun!"

Missy said, "I have learned not to dwell on the problems of being in a single-parent family but to take it as it is. I know now that I am not the only kid who has gone through it, and I don't feel all alone anymore."

Jenny said, "I found out that I could work with others and what it is like to live in a single-parent family. If I ever go into one, I would be ready."

Tom said, "I have expressed a lot of feelings (I'm starting

to sound like my mother!) that I had never told anyone about before."

Margae said, "I think I am able to express myself better and to get my feelings out into the open."

Sheri said, "I had always wanted to say, 'I have to ask my *dad*,' but it doesn't matter anymore."

Scott said, "Writing this book was a dramatic experience for me. I met people *personally* and learned that if something goes wrong, don't fret and ride it out."

Writing this book was really enjoyable. We got to meet new and interesting people, go on adventures, travel together (Hampton Beach), and share our feelings. It meant a lot to us to see the book progress, and we feel a certain group satisfaction that *we've done it!*

We think that other kids should write books about things they believe in. It is good to feel that we might have helped some other kids who are going through what we have. All in all, it has been great, and if we ever had the chance to do it again, we would.

*The
Kids' Book
About
Single-Parent
Families*

What Is a Single-Parent Family?

"My mom and dad had been fighting for about a month or so. We were living in California at the time. Finally, my mother gave up and said to us, 'In about a week or two, I am moving to Vermont. You can stay with your father, or you can go with me.' I have one brother and one sister; we all decided to go with my mom. I told myself that it really didn't matter because my dad was a workaholic and was never around anyway so we never saw him. So, one day we loaded our seven birds and two cats in the El Camino and headed for Vermont. I still wasn't sure why we were going. I knew that they weren't getting along because of all the fights they were having, but, as I said, it didn't really make a difference because we never saw my dad anyway. I was happy because my mom was happy. When we got to Vermont, I could tell that my mother was excited for her new life."

Amyee's parents separated and that was the beginning of her life in a single-parent family. Most people think of separation or divorce when they hear that someone lives in a single-parent family. That makes sense because most single-parent families are started this way. Most of us who are writing this book got into single-parent families when our parents separated and divorced.

But there are lots of other ways to get into a single-parent family. Missy's father died in a car accident when she was four years old. When Roger Sorenson was fourteen, he decided to be adopted by a single father rather than stay with his family where things weren't going well for him or them. Tina, one of the authors of this book, has a sister who decided to live alone with her grand-mother. Tanya Henckel's family became single-parent when her father went to jail. Dan Melrose's mother wanted a child without getting married or having another parent to share in his raising.

And there are families where the parents care for each other and are emotionally involved with the kids that we would also call single-parent living situations. They usually get started for work reasons, the need for more money in the family, or for educational reasons. Maya Gibson lives in one of these families. She lives with her mother and two brothers in Vermont now that her father has returned to work in Saudi Arabia for another year. Some single-parent situations get started when parents work different times of the day. Roy Statler's mother works in the daytime, and his father works at night. One of his parents is in charge while the other works, and they parent together on the weekends. More and more one parent or the other is going back to school away from home for periods of time, leaving one parent to run the household. Michael Scully's mother returned to school to be a nurse. His father man-aged the home and family.

As we were writing this book, we discovered one more way that single-parent families start that is different from all of the others. This one upset us. Sometimes you can live with both of your parents but only one of them cares about you. Chet Watkins real-ized when he was about ten years old that his father was never going to have much to do with him even though his whole family lived together. That was six years ago. "It is like talking to a wall. I have given up trying to make it different." We hope this doesn't happen much, but we think that it happens more than we know.

As you can see there are lots of ways to get into a single-parent family, and there are just as many different kinds of single-parent family living situations.

KINDS OF SINGLE-PARENT FAMILIES

One day in class we were wondering what others thought a single-parent family might be. So we decided to go out and ask people in town. The librarian said, "Kids living with their mother or their father." The clerk at the drugstore said, "One person raising a child or children alone." The police officer said, "A mother with her kids." And a reporter from the paper said, "One parent with children." They were all right, but it is even more complicated than that.

We talked a lot about what a single-parent family is. It was very hard to come to a decision. We finally agreed that the best way to describe a single-parent family was to say, "A single-parent family is any family where just one adult in the family takes care of the kids at a time." The only truly single-parent families are when a parent has a child by choice, if one parent dies, or if a parent completely disappears. Even when these things happen, we weren't sure because a kid always thinks about the missing parent.

Most kids in single-parent families live with one parent most of the time and the other parent some of the time. Tom, age thirteen, lives with his mother and visits his father every other weekend, spending longer times in the summer. Many kids share their time between parents. Dora Greven lives with her mother for two weeks and with her father for two weeks. We think that she really lives in two single-parent homes. Most kids fall somewhere in the middle, living all the time with a dad or a mom and part of the time with someone else.

Every single-parent family is different. Some work out fine for the people who live in them and some don't. There is nothing simple about the ways that single-parent families get started or how they are set up.

But then there isn't anything simple about any family nowadays.

IS THERE AN IDEAL FAMILY?

The first thing that comes to our minds when we hear about an ideal family is "The Brady Bunch" on television. On that show almost everything that happens turns out for the best. Steve, age fifteen, described it: "On that show, if one of the kids runs away, everybody is glad when he comes back." This is a nice idea, but this family is not believable. As Steve goes on to say, "If I ran away, that isn't exactly what would happen to me."

Everybody dreams of an ideal family. We all have different ideas about what they would be like. Fourteen-year-old Elizabeth gave us her idea: "I know a family that seems like the ideal family to me. The father is a gym teacher, and the mother is a school-teacher. Each of them devotes special time to the kids. They really balance each other out. They seem to do everything together: go on vacations, play games, have family discussions, and do things at home together. This family has its disadvantages: the parents are strict, and the kids aren't that independent. But I wouldn't mind a family like that."

In our dreams, we imagine that if we lived in an ideal family we would always:

Live better
Have more money
Get more love
Do more things together
Get spoiled

Everybody has a different idea of what would be ideal. Each of us had ideal families that someone else thought sounded terrible. What concerns us is that many people (including kids from single-parent families) really believe that there is *one* kind of family that is supposed to be perfect for everyone.

One day Julie B., who lives with her mother, was riding in her friend's car. "We were riding along, and my friend's mother saw a kid drinking. She said she didn't see why he drinks because he comes from a two-parent family, and his parents don't drink."

We think that most people believe that what makes a family perfect for someone is having *two* parents who live together.

We don't agree with this kind of thinking. All of us know plenty of intelligent, nice kids living in single-parent families. And we all know lots of kids from two-parent families getting into trouble. Elizabeth, who lives with her mother, brother, and sister, talked about a family she knows. "My cousins are friends with a family where the father has a great job, the mother stays home all the time, and they have money to do things with the kids. The sad thing is that their son got into drugs and became a straight-F person. The mother almost had a nervous breakdown over it, and the family started falling apart."

Everybody's family is different. A family can be any group of people who love each other. They don't have to live together, and they don't even really have to be related. A group of people can just decide to become a family. Some families have kids and some don't.

Every family has its share of joys, sorrows, downfalls, and problems. The problems might be very different. Some might have to worry about where our next paycheck is coming from and another may be concerned about "What color draperies should I choose?" The problems are different, but they may still feel like problems. Most people in a family try to cooperate to solve problems in such a way that there is a minimum of fights and arguments. But there will always be fights and arguments in any family, no matter what the problem.

What we are trying to say is that the way your family is made up won't make it a good or not so good family for you to grow up in. Just having two parents who live together won't make it perfect. Every kid needs something different from a family, and as long as you can get love and security from your family, that will be enough.

And we know that you can get it in any family, single-parent or two-parent, if the people in the family want it to happen.

WE NEVER WISHED WE WERE IN SINGLE-PARENT FAMILIES

A funny thing nowadays is that kids from two-parent families sometimes wish they were in single-parent families. This can happen when your parents have a big fight or if you are fighting with your father and, for the moment, you want to just live with your mother. We don't think that this wish is a good one. As Elizabeth told us, "I never wished I was in a single-parent family. My friends in single-parent families seemed so sad, and I didn't want that."

Although we are not sad all of the time, living in a single-parent family isn't any more or less perfect than any other family. There can be problems that go along with single-parent living that kids in other kinds of families don't have to deal with as much or any of the time. Things like:

Often less money in the house

Too much responsibility

Fights between parents who don't live together

Being without one of your parents a lot of the time

Maybe never seeing one of your parents again

Not knowing who one of your parents is

In most cases getting into a single-parent family can be very hard on a kid. And it can take a long time to get used to the lifestyle. Even Julie H., who has lived in a single-parent family since she was a year and a half, thinks so. "Adjusting has taken twelve or thirteen years. I have had to learn many things that now seem very normal. Things like my father will never come home from the office and say, 'What's for dinner?' I'm lucky if he calls me once a year to ask me stupid questions like 'How are your school grades?'

and 'Oh, by the way, what grade are you in now?' These things seem normal, but at one time they scared me half to death."

Some of us have lived in a single-parent family for a short time and some for a long time. Tina has been in one for a year, Tom for five years, and both the Julies in the group never lived in anything but a single-parent family. The rest of us fall somewhere in the middle. All of us agree that there is a lot for a kid to handle in a single-parent family. As one girl said, "There is much to sort out. Just when I think that I have it figured out and I'm on solid ground, *wham!* something changes, and I have to sort it out again."

WE WOULD HAVE A HARD TIME GOING BACK

Even though we all think about living in two-parent families for different reasons, we would find it hard to go back. Julie B. gives an example of why. "My friend has two parents who live together. One of them is home all the time. It seems like they fight all the time. It drives her crazy. She has to go out of the house just to get some time to herself. One day I was there and they had a fight over her mother cooking lunch for us and her mother was just trying to be nice. . . . My mom works from eight to five. From five to bedtime we get along just fine."

Almost everybody who gets into a single-parent family wishes what had happened to get them into it didn't happen. You never really stop thinking about your parents getting back together or a dead parent being alive again.

You do get used to living in a single-parent family though, and some kids grow to like many parts of living that way, such as:

Being more independent
Being more responsible and mature
Becoming capable
Being able to make adult kinds of decisions
Not having to listen to parents fight

Sometimes having two houses to live in
Getting very close to one parent
Knowing that you can take care of yourself
Having time to yourself

YOU AREN'T ABNORMAL

Elizabeth's uncle, a teacher, went to a teaching convention in New York City this year. One of the main topics at the convention was kids in single-parent families and their schoolwork. Speakers at the convention gave a statistic that said a majority of kids in trouble with frequent absences, cut classes, and D's and F's are from single-parent families.

When you live in a single-parent family and you hear this kind of comment, it makes you mad.

Tom, a thirteen-year-old boy who lives with his mother, brother, and sister, said, "It really depends on where people get their numbers. If the environment they are studying in is very poor, that can have a big effect. Money might have more to do with the problems than how the family is made up. You just can't tell."

The worst part is that when you hear these things about kids who live in single-parent families it makes you feel abnormal. The same thing happens when other kids or adults treat you differently, though most of the time it is adults because kids are more used to kids who live with single parents.

Some people feel sympathetic whenever you see them and say, "You poor kid." They usually ask if there is anything that they can do. Teachers you don't know very well do it also. Sometimes they ask questions like "How, when, and why?"

Kids get exasperated and angry if people treat them this way. The hardest thing for a kid is an overly sympathetic person. You want to say, "It's no big deal." Kids generally like some attention and help, but it makes them feel very bad when people keep it up.

Thinking that a kid is different isn't good for a kid. If someone thinks you're abnormal, then you can start to feel abnormal. Also, it sometimes brings back bad memories that you have worked to get under control. We think that sometimes kids act abnormal just because people think they are. We think that people act as you expect them to act. Some kids will take advantage of your sympathy and not behave. We all want to be expected to do well. Julie B. said, "I want to be expected to get straight A's and be well-behaved."

There are a lot of myths and statistics about kids in single-parent families. Some of them say that you will be more likely to:

Become a juvenile delinquent
Run away
Take drugs and get drunk
Abuse your children
Never be happy

It doesn't have to be this way.

Just because you are in a single-parent family doesn't mean that you are abnormal. You will have feelings just like anybody else —anger, love, and sorrow. You will have to deal with problems like peer pressure, alcohol, drugs, and sex as well as emotional problems related to school, family, and everyday life. Sometimes you will feel that you are different from everybody else. The important thing is to just hang in there and take the problems one day at a time.

All of us have made it that way.

WHY WE ARE WRITING THIS BOOK

Writing this book has been very exciting. All of us have enjoyed the chance to talk and learn about life in single-parent families and what it means for a kid. Writing the book has made us feel good because we are doing something for others, making our parents proud of us, and making our brothers and sisters jealous!

Most important, though, is that more and more kids are living in single-parent families now. A lot of kids feel lost after a separation or the death of a parent, especially when parents don't help kids to understand what is happening in their lives. Many kids feel guilty and sad when the change happens. Tina suggested, "A lot of kids out in the world need help and feel very lonely. They need something to get them through the hard times of divorce, death, or whatever the situation." Many of us wished that we had a book like this one when we were starting out in single-parent families.

We want kids to know that a single-parent family is just another kind of family and that just as in any family there will be:

Love
Money problems
Fun
Chores to be done
Good times
Bad times
Fights with your brothers and sisters

Getting used to living in a single-parent family can sometimes happen fast and sometimes take a long time. We would like to help kids to accept the fact that they are in a single-parent family and to be satisfied with single-parent living. And, as Elizabeth said, "Living in a single-parent family can be fun. You only need to learn how to make it that way."

A lot of us in the group had all sorts of feeling about living in single-parent families that we had never talked about when we first started writing this book. Kids today try to hide their feelings and act tough. When you do, it can make you feel bad inside and sometimes different from everybody else, like something is wrong with you. Some of our relatives and friends living in single-parent families feel this way.

By sharing thoughts and experiences of our own and of people we interviewed while writing this book, we think we can help kids with different feelings and experiences who consider themselves abnormal. We want to show them that their thoughts and feelings are *normal* and that they aren't alone.

Kids need to know that when they get into a single-parent family everything is not going to be the same, but it will be all right.

2

The First Week

"Most people say that divorce tears a family apart. My parents have just gotten a divorce, and it didn't even affect our family at all! You know how a lot of parents fight and hate each other during a divorce? Well, my parents were really neat; it seems as if they are still married. The only difference is that Dad doesn't live at home anymore. None of us cried or anything like that, and Mom took it really well. She still does! We just all go on like nothing happened. Mom even says that they might get back together again. She doesn't know how soon, but they are dating and things look great!"

To tell the truth, we made this story up. This sounds just ideal, doesn't it? All of us would love to have started our lives in single-parent families this way. Unfortunately . . .

None of *our* first weeks went this well. And we can't really imagine any that would start out this way. (Of course, anything is possible.) We did find when we interviewed people that some first weeks are better than others or maybe just not quite as bad.

From a kid's point of view, the first week is often, as Ellen Foster said, *"Havoc.* The phone keeps ringing and people keep calling and wanting to know what happened and why. Everyone gets the story mixed up. One person would say this and another would say that. Then another would tell it entirely differently! Everyone kept asking questions. Sometimes *you* wouldn't even know what happened because the story would get so turned around."

We are convinced, from our experiences and from others, that you can get used to living in a single-parent family and learn to like it. But not necessarily right away.

We talked and talked about our first weeks in single-parent families. We thought about things like:

How they began

How our parents handled themselves

How friends and relatives reacted

How we felt and what we did

All first weeks are a little different, and yours is probably different from ours. We all think that the first week in a single-parent family may feel like the longest that you will ever spend!

WHY WE ARE WRITING ABOUT THE FIRST WEEK

We are writing about the first week, even though it may be the saddest time for us, to make it a little easier for you (and us) to talk or think about it.

The first week in a single-parent family usually brings so much confusion into your life. Things are changing in the first week that are very important parts of your life. You have to start becoming more independent immediately. Most of the time only one parent is around, and since this is a hard time for them, they might not be available. It can be very lonely because when you want to talk to your parents they aren't always there. The first week can bring many strong feelings and memories that you don't understand.

Kids often block them out of their minds because the memories are too painful and they don't think they can handle them. Sometimes you do this on purpose. Tina, whose parents separated, said, "The first week (for some kids) is such a depressing period in your life that you try not to remember or think about the bad things that happened."

Sometimes you block memories out without knowing it. We

call this having a mental block. What we mean is that you carry the memories of what happened but don't want to recall them. And sometimes by not wanting to recall them, you really and truly can't.

Another reason that you block them out might be that you were, like some of us, too young to really know what was going on. This can be a problem for a kid because you *do* have memories, but they are usually, as Scott says, "in bits and pieces and all out of order." Because of this you could walk around for the rest of your life with feelings that you don't understand or beliefs about what happened that aren't true. This could really affect how you feel about yourself.

Even though it is possible to block these memories and feelings out of your mind, we don't think you ever forget them. As Laura, one of the authors said, "You can hide your feelings just so long and then, *pop!*" Getting them out in the open with someone important and safe to you or maybe just to yourself can be helpful.

Of course, just because we are saying this, you shouldn't run out and tell your life story to someone. Blocking bad memories out is useful sometimes especially if those memories are really upsetting, like if you have been beaten or raped. If you haven't talked about it (or maybe even thought about it) before, you probably have good reasons. It may be because it is too painful for you or you haven't found the right person to share it with.

Many of us took *years* to begin talking about the first week and asking questions about it, so there is no rush. But what most of us believe is that you do want to talk about it to somebody important, like a parent, brother, sister, boyfriend, or girlfriend, and that talking about it, even if it hurts, can make you feel better in the long run.

WE KNOW THAT THIS SOUNDS BAD!

We were worried that the first week would sound *so* depressing that you wouldn't want to know anymore about being in a single-parent family. Or, if you were just going through your first week in a single-parent family, you might be *too* frightened of what was ahead for you. So there are some things that we think you should know right now!

It Isn't Always Awful

Everybody's first week isn't completely awful. Elizabeth said, "It is true that in the first week all your feelings may seem to be a mess and that this can feel very scary. But some parents handle the first week in such a way as to keep those feelings to a minimum. When my parents first separated, I saw my dad every week, and we stayed very close. Our whole family still went places together. Everything was confusing but less so than if my dad hadn't been around."

The move to single-parent life is going to mean something different for everyone. Sure, if your parents separate or if one of them dies, it is bad. And, although it can feel bad if parents leave for a time and aren't as available to you, it doesn't always affect your feelings of security. When Maya's father went back to work overseas, she wasn't worried that he wasn't going to love her. He contacted her regularly, and she knew where she could reach him. When Michael's mother went back to school to be a nurse, he was a little concerned, but also he was excited for his mom and for the family. Even when Chris and Matt Mole's parents separated, they never doubted that both their parents loved them.

And It Can Be a Relief

From our experience, nobody really wants a parent to leave or die (except in really *special* cases). But there are times when, even if you don't want the change, that first week brings a sigh of relief.

Knowing that a change is coming can sometimes be worse than the change itself. This is especially true when one of your parents has been very, very sick for a long time, and you know that he or she may die. As Tom said, "Every night you go to bed and wonder whether they are going to be there the next day." Scott told us about one of his relatives: "I watched my uncle die. It was very hard. He was in so much pain. Every time that he heard a siren, he would be afraid that someone was coming to take him to the hospital to be treated. He didn't want to leave his home. When he finally died, it was better. He had been in pain for so long, and then he wasn't anymore."

Parents separating can mean the end of fighting. And we all say, *"We can't stand the fighting!"* It drives kids crazy. Sometimes you find yourself, as Sheri said, "praying for a divorce just to end the fighting."

It seems that when parents are reaching the end of their relationship or before any major change, the fighting can go on day and night. Sometimes the fighting is constant quiet tension, but more often it is loud and mean. It is scary for a kid. A girl in our school said, "I hated it when things would go flying across the room. I was worried that one day my mom and dad would get into a big fight and really hurt us. Sometimes I would step in and say, 'Cut it out!' "

Another time you might feel relief is when a stepparent is gone. Stepfamily living has unavoidable conflicts built into it, we think maybe more than any other type of family. Warren Allen, an adult we interviewed, told us what it was like when his stepfather died. "It was sad because I was finally beginning to see him as a person, but in a way a relief. It simplified my life immensely and a little for my mother, too. My parents had divorced when I was little. After my mother remarried, I shut my stepfather out for almost all my childhood and adolescent years. We used to get in all kinds of conflicts about what kids wear and the right way to do things. It drove me crazy because, in my mind, he wasn't my real father and didn't have the right to tell me what to do."

Also, it's usually the second time around for getting into a single-parent family, and you aren't quite as shocked. You have some ideas about how to handle it and what to do. You are still frustrated and confused, but you are more able to "count to ten and try to calm yourself down." You might even have an "oh no, here we go again" feeling.

We aren't saying that kids don't care about the stepparent. For many kids, the stepparent *is* their parent, and they love and need him or her. Rachael J. Fortney, whom we interviewed, had this to say: "I want my stepfather to adopt me. He treats me like any other daughter. I want him to be there in case anything ever happens to my mother so that I can stay with my family."

We do think that many stepparents and kids don't get as attached to each other. Noel, whose mother and stepfather broke up when she was nine, said, "He had never legally adopted me or anything and in many ways life was easier after he left. I still wanted to see him. I was afraid that he wouldn't come to see me, and he didn't. He had plenty of chances. My mom would let him come, but he always made promises that he didn't keep. My mom finally told him to stay away from me."

There might be relief at home right away if the parent who left is alcoholic. Alcoholic parents are unpredictable. They can become violent easily and don't take good care of the kids. One girl whose parents separated when she was a baby said, "When I was a year old, my mother decided she couldn't take my father anymore. He was alcoholic. He would go out every night, and sometimes he wouldn't come home. When he did come home, it wasn't worth it. He would always have a hangover, and he would always yell at my mother. He wasn't a responsible person. Once he was watching me and left the house because he needed a drink. My mom happened to come home and found me alone in the playpen. That was when she decided to leave."

And you are always worrying about them. What bar are they in? Will the police call tonight? How will they act when they get home? Will they get into an accident? Your worry can become real, too. Debby Lowell said, "One night my mother and father had a big fight because it was his birthday, and he wanted to go out and get drunk. My mom wouldn't go. So my dad went out by himself and got into an accident and died."

When you are a kid and your parent gets drunk all the time,

not having that parent around is a relief. But you need to remember, as Noel says, "You really don't want the parent to go away, just the alcohol."

You Get Past the Bad Times

If the first week is very bad for you and the people around you, it probably won't *always* be that way. We know because many of us had upsetting things happen to us, but we made it this far. You just need to remember, as Elizabeth said, "Most of the time, if things get very bad, they have to get better."

And it can get bad sometimes. Just how bad or how good your first week is will depend on things like:

How your first week started

How the people around you reacted

What the change meant to you

HOW IT STARTED

The things that cause families to become single-parent families are separation (and in the end, divorce); death of a parent; a parent going off to work or school; or a parent choosing to become a parent through adoption, foster care, or birth.

But what exactly happened to begin your life in a single-parent family? Also, was it a total surprise? Did you have some clues that something was about to happen? Or, did you know about it well ahead of time? We think that all these things make a difference in how the first week feels to a kid.

Out of the Blue

"One day my mother and I went for a ride by my father's work (he worked nights) because my mother had been told that my father was seeing someone else who also worked nights. My mother said, 'I won't believe it until I see it.' Well, we rode by there and saw them together. (I was shocked and so was my mother!) We went home and the next day my mother and father had this really big fight and decided to separate."—Tanya, age fourteen.

"When I was four years old, my father went out one night. While he was driving, his car went over a bank. He got out okay, but when he climbed back up to the road to get help, he got hit by an ex-cop who was drunk. My dad was killed. The police came to the door and told us."—Missy, age fifteen.

We think that these are the hardest ways to begin single-parent families because *nobody* has time to plan, and everybody is shocked. As Noel says, "This kind of change blows your mind. You can't change it because you have no control over what has happened. And you can't ask anyone else to change it, either, because they don't have any more control than you. Everyone just feels helpless. One day you feel fine and the next day, *boom!*"

The best way we have to describe these kinds of things is "They rot."

We Had Some Clues

"At first my dad wasn't coming home that much. Then he started not coming home at night. I never saw him! I suspected that he was seeing someone else. I was right. One day my mom told me that she and Dad weren't getting along that well. She said that Dad was moving out, and they were going to get a divorce. I wasn't surprised."—Ellen, age fifteen.

Kids, even very little kids, can have an uncanny sense about what goes on in a family. Adults don't always realize it, but it's true! A lot of parents think that they can protect kids from the truth. This would be nice, but it rarely happens. As Scott says, "Sometimes you know something is going on. You may just have a sense that something is wrong. You might not even be able to put it into words, but you know."

Different clues kids pick up are:

Parents' behavior changes

Relatives and friends talk about "the situation"

Parents pretend nothing is going on when you ask them

People stop talking when you come into a room

Parents fight more than usual

Parents cry all the time

Many times you don't realize that the clues were clues until later on. These memories float around in your head like pieces of a jigsaw puzzle. Only in retrospect do you realize that they were clues at all. It might take you months to put these pieces together.

We think that you are just a little more ready for the change because you prepare yourself, sometimes without knowing it. You do things like daydream, "I wonder what it would be like if my parents got separated." You might even find yourself wishing that they would separate. One girl from our school decided that "no matter what happens, I'm not going to lose my cool." (Of course, you *do* lose your cool.)

Having clues, even if you don't understand their meaning right away, is usually easier than when the change comes out of nowhere. When the clues do fall into place, you go "Oh, yeah." You feel comforted if you can make sense out of the confusion.

When You Know in Advance

"My mother was sick a long time. She had cancer for about ten years. When she died, it wasn't a big surprise. My dad was an Episcopal minister, and he was really good with us. He helped us to express our feelings and understand what was going on."— Bronwen Sherwin, age nineteen.

"We had lived in Saudi Arabia for about eight years. We knew about a year ago that there was a chance my dad would stay on one more year to complete his work. He is the chief horticulturist for the King Faisal Hospital. The rest of the family was to return to the States so my brother could go to school (schools in Saudi Arabia only go to the ninth grade.) It was a hard decision for all of us. My father made some attempts to find a position in the States but in the end made the choice to go back to Saudi Arabia for the year." —Maya, age seventeen.

For the most part, we think that the changes kids know about ahead of time are the best. That way you may be more able to get the help and answers when you need them. You have some time to prepare.

Some kids have parents who talk to them about changes that are happening in a family to help them understand. These parents know that kids often handle big changes best when they know what's going to happen. Bronwen's parents talked to her for years before her mother was going to die of cancer and helped her with her feelings by encouraging her to talk. Michael's mother, who went back to school in another city, planned ahead with the kids, and so did Chris and Matt's parents before they separated. All of these kids said that talking about the change made the first week much easier than it would have been.

But talking and planning doesn't make the first week trouble-free. As Tom said, "Just because I knew that my parents were going to separate, that doesn't mean I was ready for it. Until my dad actually left, it was all just talk. You don't *really* think that it is going to happen." Also, it is possible to know about a change, like a move or a separation, and not really agree with it. As Maya said, "I was angry at my parents for not working it out so that we could stay together. None of us really wanted to be split up. I think that my dad didn't really believe that we wouldn't be there."

We agree with Noel, who said, "Even if you have some idea that your parents are going to divorce or if one of them is sick and might die, you are never really prepared for the situation to go that far."

As you can see, there are lots of different kinds of events that start single-parent families. The event itself can be hard enough, but what seems to matter as much is how people around react and handle themselves.

THE PEOPLE IN YOUR LIFE

When you get hurt, you think, "this is just happening to me." But it isn't. Every change in one person in a family does something to everyone else, sometimes in a big way and sometimes in a small way. The way they react will affect how *you* feel, and what you do will affect how *they* feel. And it keeps going around and around.

The Parent You Stay with

We actually think that the first week in a single-parent family is more distressing for the parent who remains at home than it is for the kids. Darcey explained, "The parent at home has to do everything—get babysitters, pay bills, and get a better job. Also, that parent doesn't have another adult to talk to about the way they feel deep inside. A kid can talk to a parent, but a parent can't tell a kid. A kid can't talk seriously with a parent the way the other parent did. Remember, they slept together and miss being next to that parent in bed." It may mean the end of a relationship that they worked very hard at for a long time. We think that this is true regardless of which parent wanted the change and that most parents:

Cry and seem depressed
Don't eat right
Drink more
Smoke too much
Bite their nails

There were a lot of tears the first week. Laura said, "I remember the first big meal that we had. It was on Christmas Eve. Everybody was together except my mom and dad. It was really hard because everybody was there holding hands and having a good time and my father was sitting there crying." Missy remembers, after her father's death. "Well, when my relatives came home from the funeral, my mom kept breaking down. They were scared that she might end up in the hospital."

Sometimes parents are so upset that their eating habits change. Tanya told us, "In the first week after my parents separated, my mom stopped eating and began to lose weight. I got most worried the night we were all sitting around eating strawberry shortcake, and she didn't have a piece." Tom's mother "brought home a whole bunch of junk food." (Actually, he thought it was great!)

They might even start drinking or taking other drugs to hide the hurt. This can be the worst because you don't know how they are going to react. One girl we interviewed had this to say: "I remember seeing my father drink. I would hide the booze from him, and he would get mad at me. Sometimes he would come home drunk and start throwing things. I would try to explain to him that I loved him and didn't want him to drink."

They can seem to be in a fog. They seem lost, short-tempered, and lonely. You might even wonder if they know what they are doing. Mike Parker remembers, "No one talked for the first week. The only time anyone did speak was to ask for food or money. My dad was very nervous. He kept doing things like buying me the same thing over and over again. By the end of the week, I owned at least five matchbox cars—all the same kind. Also, he kept forgetting where he was. Sometimes he would wake up in the morning and think that he was still living at home and freak out when he realized that he wasn't." In the middle of the shock and confusion, parents sometimes make big, sudden decisions as a way of handling their feelings. Tina remembers, "One day I came home from school, and my mother said, 'Pack your bags, we're moving to Florida.' It was scary because we hardly knew anybody there and she hadn't even talked to me about it." Every parent doesn't react this quickly and in such a big way.

And often parents feel angry. This is especially true if they have been abandoned by the other parent. They can have these feelings even if they were part of the decision. These are things they may be angry about:

Being rejected

Handling the family alone

Doing things which frighten them

During this week, parents need attention (a lot of hugging). They need comfort from us. This can be hard because of our own feelings, but most kids, as Tina says, "love and care for their parents," so we do it.

When parents cry and get upset, you feel, as one girl said, "helpless and hopeless." Even though you feel this way, we think they should be able to cry. As Elizabeth stated, "We would be more worried if they didn't get upset." Noel, whose mother and stepfather separated and later divorced, told us: "It is hard to watch a parent get upset, but it is right then that they really need you. It is important to let a parent cry so that they can get their feelings out."

Of course, parents are not always unhappy that they are on their own. In some cases they are actually glad and relieved. This is especially true if they have been mistreated by the parents who are now gone. One of us had a cousin whose mother was happy when his father left. He said, "My mom had really been abused by my dad. And when he left, all that stopped."

There are situations, too, as Tom said, "where parents never really get along but have stayed together for reasons like money or for the sake of the kids. When they finally break up, it is more of a relief than a misery because now they can go on with living the way that they want." Scott, whose parents separated, said, "It was kind of like that for my parents. I don't even remember them fighting that much. But I do remember them having different ideas about everything. If my dad would say yes, my mother would say no."

The Parent You Are Not with

We think that parents who are not with the family can have many of the same feelings as parents who are with you. They have just gone through a change, too and probably feel sad, lonely, confused, angry, or relieved for many of the same reasons.

There are some differences though. They don't have the responsibility of running the family, and they don't have the benefits either. The biggest difference is that they feel left out. We think that this is so no matter why they aren't part of the family (even if it seems to a kid that they don't care at the time). Maya said, "I think that my dad was hurt and surprised that we didn't choose to go to Saudi Arabia with him."

Parents can act very funny when they get these feelings. As Sheri says, "They might get very attentive to the kids. They may take them on special trips or buy them lots of presents to make sure that their kids will still care for them." Sometimes it can get very bad because your parents might try to use you to get to the other parent. Elizabeth said, "They come to you and cry and beg you to talk to the other parent, or they might lay a guilt trip on you and get you to take their side." We think that these parents are afraid that they are going to lose their kids and their families.

Sometimes parents just don't contact the family at all. Some just don't know that kids need to hear from a parent no matter what happens. Other times they are so resentful of being left out that they stay away to punish everyone, kids included. Or if *they* were the ones who wanted to be apart from the family, they feel ashamed to come around or call.

Brothers and Sisters

The first week in a single-parent family can bring out the best and the worst in brothers and sisters.

A lot of times brothers and sisters realize right away that they need to work together. They know when a parent is down, and they really pull together to help out. Elizabeth said, "For the first couple of days, we were close. We really tried not to fight." And Missy, after her father died, said, "We tried to work together; we knew this was a time when our mother needed everyone."

You are surprised by how capable you are. All of a sudden you find that you can:

Clean up
Make meals
Do laundry
Take care of yourself
Even (ugh!) get along with your brothers and sisters

But at times it can go the other way, maybe even in the same week. The pressure of the change, whatever it is, can cause brothers and sisters to fight.

Norman said that after his father left, *"everybody* was fighting." Brothers and sisters often have different opinions of what happened. Tanya said, "All my sisters were glad that my dad left, even though I wasn't. They had some terrible feelings toward my father for how much he hurt my mother."

Sometimes, when there is a lot of hurt and confusion, it can get very bad. One boy said, "It was terrible; we fought like cats and dogs." Another kid we interviewed said, "My sister and brother fought more than ever. My brother even hit my mother, and he never did that before. I thought that he was going to kill her."

And kids blame each other, too. Darcey describes a typical situation: "They might get into arguments and start saying things like 'You made her do it. If it wasn't for you Mom wouldn't have left. You were always bugging her.' "

Often older kids in single-parent families have to take over caring for younger brothers and sisters. This can be a help to the older kids because it gives them something to think about. One girl said, "In a way, I didn't have time to think about what was happening to me. I had to handle it because my little brother and sister needed me to help them."

Sometimes though this can be too much for kids who are upset and used to having adults around. Julie B., who was little when her parents separated, remembers, "In the first week my brother and sister had to take care of me. I was really young. They got into a big fight inside the house. My sister hit my brother with a candlestick. While all this was going on, I just started walking down the street all by myself. One of our neighbors found me, took me back to the house, and called my mom at work."

Even if you are fighting in the first week, you are glad to have brothers and sisters around. Sometimes it is the start of a much closer relationship with them (even if it seems like the end of a good one).

Friends and Relatives

"As soon as I found out that my parents were separating, I called my best friend and said, 'Guess what? My parents are getting a divorce.' It was nice that my friend was there."—Elizabeth.

You really find out how important people around you are in

the first week in a single-parent family. A lot of times they become the difference between being okay and not okay.

Missy said that after her father died, "Everyone around us was very helpful and always came to visit us. They made sure that we had everything we needed." Tina had the same experience when her parents separated. "My friends *immediately* tried to help in any way that they could. It was really nice to know that I had some people I could turn to. I even remember one boy in school who I really didn't know too well. He saw me crying one day and came over to help me out. It really meant a lot to me."

It's good to have people besides your family around when you are feeling so bad. They can say things to you that you can't say to yourself right then. Things like:

We're sorry

We love you and don't want you to feel bad

You will make it

It isn't your fault

Even though you appreciate and need people in that first week, letting people know what has happened to you, even very best friends, is not the easiest thing to do. You are having such a hard time with your feelings that you can't stand the thought of talking to anyone. As Norman said, "Right after my father died, I didn't say anything to anybody, and nobody said anything to me. I didn't *want* anybody to talk to me because I just had too many feelings. I remember running into my dad's best friend. He said, 'How is your dad?' I was pretty upset. I stood there and couldn't answer. Finally, I just turned around and left. He thought I was mad at him or something."

Although you don't feel like telling anyone what happened, it is sometimes better than waiting for them to ask you. When you do tell them, you are more prepared for talking about it and less likely to be caught off guard. Usually, when people hear that a parent has left or died, they are shocked and surprised. They might even be so sad that you need to help *them* out. You may have to, as Darcey said, "let them know that it isn't the end of the world, even though it seems like it."

Also, Margae felt that "it is better for people to hear it right from you instead of from someone else. That way they know it is really true and not just a rumor." Of course, you might think to yourself, "Let them read it in the paper."

We do think it is important to be careful because it is very easy to get your feelings hurt in that first week. Scott said, "You really have to pay attention to the personality of the person who you are telling and not tell people who will tease you or hurt you. Sometimes kids misunderstand and think that you are just trying to get them to feel sorry for you. This can be one of the biggest reasons that kids don't tell anyone because they are afraid of this." We found that some kids won't go to school right away just to avoid this happening.

And people do say things that really upset you, sometimes on purpose but more likely without knowing it. These are some of the remarks that might seem crazy to you:

"Don't cry because she is not coming back. It happens to a lot of people."

"He was a good man, but your mom is better off without him." (As Elizabeth says, "Things can slip out if the person you are talking to didn't like your parent.")

"You will live!"

"They will get back together."

"Don't worry." *(Of course you are going to worry!)*

And people can do things that really hurt. For example, they get mad at each other. Norman said, "After my aunts and uncles found out that my parents were breaking up, they started fighting, too. Some tried to get my parents back together; everybody took sides. It turned into an all-out war."

Or even worse, if one of your parents has died, people around you can start arguing over your parent's stuff. Sometimes things that were meaningful to you get taken without your even being asked. Bronwen told us, "After my mother died, someone took my favorite piece of my mother's jewelry. But I still have her ring and little things that were important to her, like her garden."

Scott said, "If it is a greedy family, they might all start fighting over the will." Margae, one of the authors, remembers, "After my aunt died, people would come up and say things like, 'Oh, we'll take this or we'll take that.' We hadn't even made the arrangements yet. People couldn't wait." This makes you sad because the person is hardly gone from your life.

However, we know that most people are really trying to be helpful. Believe us, in that first week when everything is upside down, we appreciate them even if we can't always understand what they are doing. One thing we are sure of is that, as Tina says, "Once you tell people who are important to you, they can understand and be of help to you." And we also think you can be of help to each other.

FIRST—WEEK FEELINGS

As you can see, the first week in a single-parent family can mean that you lose a lot of control over your life.

We tried to decide how to answer the question "What is the most common feeling that kids have in the first week in a single-parent family?" We came up with a lot of different answers. Michelle said sadness, Scott said fury, and Amyee said relief. Others of us said things like guilt, loneliness, and even happiness. We talked about all of these, we even argued about it. What we decided was that, in the first week there are *so* many changes and *so* many things going on, it is possible to feel all of them at once!

Of course, we don't think that you *have* to feel all of them. Some of us felt some and not others. It really depends on who you are, what happened to you, and how old you were. If you were real young, like a baby, you wouldn't know what was happening. If you were older than five, you would be more aware of your feelings but not be able to completely understand what the change was about. If you were older than eleven, you would have both strong feelings and be able to understand what was happening.

So these are some of the feelings that we felt and why. Maybe you had some others.

Shock

When you feel too much at once, you can be in shock. Shock is a funny thing; it's hard to describe. Another good word for shock is "stunned." We thought about "surprised" as another way to describe shock, but it is more than surprised.

Shock can happen to you when there is a sudden big change in your life. It could happen if someone gave you a million dollars. But this isn't the kind of shock that we are talking about. The kind we are describing comes from the fear of not knowing what is going to happen next and whether or not you believe you can handle all the big feelings that go with it.

Everybody doesn't go into shock. The older you are and the more you are prepared for the change, the less likely you are to feel shock. But even these things won't keep you from going into shock.

You can tell you are in shock when:

You are totally spacey
People talk to you, but you don't hear them
You sit and stare at a flower for a long time
You read a page without reading it
You are afraid of everything without knowing why
You cry for no particular reason
All of the above

Most kids just want to be by themselves when they are in shock. The only things you can think about are your problems, if you can think at all, and you want time to sort them out. Tom, after his parents separated, said, "I stayed at my grandparents' house a lot. That was where my dad was living at the time. It was pretty good staying there because they were around to talk to but at work most of the time. I just wanted to be alone and think about what was going on. I was so young and confused." Debby felt the same way after her father died. She said, "I just wanted to be left alone and not have anyone bother me."

You can get very cranky when you are in shock. Many of us did. Debby said, "I would just want to stay up in my room. Whenever my mother would come up, I would yell, 'Stay away from me!' " We think you do this because you might be angry or you don't want people telling you what to feel. Other kids might stay away from home or try to stick with friends so they don't have to think about it or talk about it.

Parents and friends don't always understand when this happens to you. Some will think that you are:

Moping around
Going crazy
On drugs

When you are in shock, you just need time. We think that if you can find someone safe to talk with that you are better off. But as we said, *you* have to decide what is best for you. However, if you're getting sick, not eating for a long time, or thinking about hurting yourself, then you may not be able to judge what would be best for you. If people around you are trying to help you, you should let them.

Fear

Shock is often caused by fear. And in the first week, there can be many fears. Your head can get filled with questions like "Why me and my family? Why did it have to happen to us?" or "What will happen now? Will we have to change?" If your parents are as shocked by the change or scared by the future as you, they might react in a way that worries you.

In the first week, parents cry a lot. Jean Haynes, the mother of one of the authors, was also from a single-parent family. Her father died when she was fifteen. "It was very hard for my mother. She cried night after night. I used to hear it from my bed." Kids don't like their parents to cry. You feel frightened, and it makes you think that everything is not going to be okay.

For some reason, too, it is harder to watch a man cry than a woman. We think that men should cry, but as Margae said, "It gets drummed into your head that women cry because they are weak and men don't because they are strong." We don't believe this, but the truth is that it is more upsetting to see a father cry than a mother.

You tend to be most concerned about the parent at home with you. You are afraid that the parent won't be able to take care of you and might leave or die. Amyee said, "I was afraid that I would have to live in an orphanage." This seems silly, looking back, but it really can happen. Faith remembered a friend's situation. "My friend's parents got a divorce. Her mother was so upset that she had a nervous breakdown and had to be put in the hospital. The girl was put in a foster home." Luckily, this doesn't happen very much.

Sometimes they are so upset that you don't know what they are going to do. You worry that they might try to hurt themselves. You might be sitting there watching television and all of a sudden they say something like "I think I just want to die." Most parents won't commit suicide, but every kid worries that they might.

You are also concerned whether or not the parent who is out of the house is safe, will ever see you again, or still loves you. You even get concerned for a parent who has died. One girl we talked to said, "I hoped that my dad was okay in the cold hard ground."

All these fears go away with time. Most parents make it through just as we did, and most parents come back to see you. But until you can talk to them or someone else about the change, one question sometimes goes through your head: "Is it all my fault?"

Guilt

Probably one of the biggest feelings that you might have is that *you did it.* You can feel this way for a number of reasons. Usually, it is because you are too young and you think that you can do almost anything.

Scott put it into words when he said, "Kids blame themselves for what has happened to them. They can see logic everywhere around them. They can come up with reasons why it is not their parents' fault or anybody else's, but when they look at themselves, they can't be so reasonable. You have to remember that to a kid almost anything is possible."

And it is hard to imagine that adults are human and make mistakes. Julie H. said, "It is much easier to think that you are at fault than a parent. And you don't really want to accept the fact that a parent is gone so you say things to yourself like 'If I hadn't done this or if I had done that.'" One girl we interviewed even blamed herself for her father's death in a car accident. She said, "If I had only kept him from going out that night."

Kids are used to getting blamed by their parents for doing things wrong anyway. Sheri, whose parents separated when she was young, said, "Kids are impressionable. Let's say that a mother is angry and yelling. She doesn't have to be yelling at you, but you will think that she is angry with you."

You really can get blamed sometimes. Tessie Black remembers, "In the first week my mother was so mad that she would scream at us kids. 'It is all your fault because you kids were always fighting. If it wasn't for you we wouldn't have broken up.' The hard part about this is that you never really forget what was said and that can hurt."

Not everybody does feel guilty. It seems if parents make sure that kids know they didn't have anything to do with the change, kids don't take it out on themselves. We know two brothers, Chris and Matt, whose parents spent a lot of time talking to them before they separated. They must have done a good job because Chris couldn't believe that kids could ever think it was their fault.

If you do feel like it's your fault, well, it isn't. We know from experience that just telling you it is not your fault won't make you believe it. All we can say is that we went through it.

Anger

We think that people feel anger whenever they have to make a change they don't want. Noel said, "People don't like big changes and will do almost anything to avoid them." This is just as true for kids as it is for adults. You can be angry about many things and with many people. Mostly, though, what makes you mad has to do with one of your parents being gone.

A kid can get angry whenever a parent leaves, no matter what the reason or for how long. As Tom says, "Kids need their parents. They need them for a lot of reasons, like to give them advice when they are stuck. The most important reason, though, is that kids need to always know that someone cares about them." And as Sheri says, "Your parents are part of you. You really rely on them, and when they go out the door, a part of you goes with them."

The worst situation is when parents leave and don't let you know where they are or when and if you will see them again. Julie H., whose father left and didn't return said, "You feel hurt and angry because they didn't tell you. You start to feel resentment, too. You feel like you and the parent who has stayed have gotten used. You get so mad that you start to fantasize that the parent who has left is deathly sick or even dead and gone from you forever."

You can even get mad at a parent for dying. This might make you feel guilty, but it happens. You should try not to be surprised or feel bad. A lot of kids have the thought "How could they go and leave us?" As we said, kids don't like it when a parent leaves.

Sometimes, after one of your parents has gone, you find yourself mad at the parent who is home. Margae was reminded of this when she read one of Judy Blume's books, called *Tiger Eyes*. "It described a girl whose father had been shot. The girl felt angry because her mother became numb and stopped being a parent to her. She wanted her mother to provide her with guidance and help her make decisions that she didn't know how to make." You might feel selfish if this happens to you, but it's natural.

Also, you might blame the parent you are with for the other parent's going. Norman thought that it was his mother's fault because his father was gone. "I was mad at her for throwing him out of the house. I wanted her to give him one more chance, but she wouldn't." After her father was killed, Debby was mad at her mother. "I thought, 'If only she had kept him home that night.'"

You might even find yourself angry at both of your parents at once. When parents separate, you are angry that they couldn't work out their problems so that the family could stay together. Or you get mad at them for pulling you back and forth between them.

One parent or the other can tell you bad things about the other parent, as Laura said, "to try to win you on their side." Sheri said, "This makes you so confused. Parents need to remember that, just because parents aren't good for each other, it doesn't mean they will be bad for you." The worst thing that happens is your parents ask you questions like "Who do you want to live with, Mom or Dad?" or "Who do you love more?"

There are a lot of different reasons to get angry in that first week. We don't think that any of them are right or wrong. If you get angry, you get angry.

Of course, when we all have time to think about it, the things that happened really aren't anybody's fault; they just happened. But right at the moment, when everything is in an uproar, it is hard to think straight. And sometimes it is easier to be angry than to feel all the sadness.

Sadness

Behind all the other feelings that you are having in the first week, if you are like us at all, is a feeling of sadness. You notice it most at special times of the day and in little things that are missing from the house.

Mealtime is often the worst. This is when, even when things were hardest at home, the whole family would sit down together. In the first week, it changes fast. Elizabeth said, "It is no longer a family affair. It becomes just grabbing something to eat." And Tina says, "It becomes so lonely and depressing. You usually just eat out or make your own meals. It is usually quick and not nutritious at all."

Five o'clock can be bad, too. Debby, whose father died, remembered what it meant to her. "That was when my dad would come home. I would sit there and stare at the door waiting for him to come through. But he never did."

Sometimes it is the little things that are gone. Derek said, "The house can seem so empty. Pictures can be missing, maybe your favorites." Elizabeth remembers what she first noticed. "The biggest change was that my dad's great big black chair was gone. I used to curl up in it all the time, it was my favorite."

You are sad because you somehow know that life will not be the same. It might be going to get better, but in that first week, most kids can't know. All you know is that you had hoped it would get better. And now you are just wondering, "Why won't the time go by so that the pain will go away?"

WHAT KIDS NEED IN THE FIRST WEEK

We know that the first week is a difficult one for everybody and that you can't expect parents to always be able to give kids all the attention that they might need right away. But we are afraid that when adults are having problems kids often get lost in the shuffle.

There are some really important things that kids need in the first week that we think are possible for parents and other adults to give us. They are:

To have the change explained as clearly as possible

To be told that it isn't the kids' fault

To know where both parents are

To have some contact with each of the parents

To be left out of parents' fighting

To understand that a kid might feel different from the way an adult feels

To know that people around care

We think that it is important for kids to understand what is happening in their lives. The more that they know, the better that they can handle whatever change is happening. Of course, they don't need to know every little detail, just the facts with no excuses. Kids know when they are being lied to or not being told something important. We think that even when something is bad, like a parent being sick enough to die or one parent leaving for good, kids deserve to know.

This doesn't mean that they aren't going to have feelings about it—anger, sadness, whatever. But when you know as best you can what is going to happen next, you feel safe and steady.

Kids need to know that what is happening isn't their fault. And they really need to hear it from adults around them, those who are staying and those who are going. Even though adults are upset in the first week (and maybe longer), they need to remember that some things that are said never really are forgotten.

The worst thing that parents can do is go off and leave their kids without letting them know where they will be and when they will see them again. The absolute worst is never to return again. As we will talk about later, this hurts you forever in some way. We know many kids who don't like themselves because one of their parents abandoned them. And even if a parent is not going to leave forever, he or she should know that kids feel much safer if they know *when* and *where* they are going to see or hear from the parent. It makes a great big difference.

Kids don't like parents fighting anytime. One of the harder kinds of fighting that goes on is when parents pull back and forth on the kids and don't deal with each other. As a kid, you have to pass messages back and forth like "Tell your father to pick you up at ten and not before." Or you have to listen to one parent criticizing the other one. This is very hard because most of the time you love them both. And the worst line of all is "You are just like your. . . ." If a parent has something bad to say about the other parent, he or she could start by saying, "This is my opinion, you can have your own." We know that there is fighting in every relationship and that there may need to be fighting to have a good relationship. But kids need to live their own lives and shouldn't have to get involved in adults' arguments.

Kids need to be respected for their own feelings in the first week. They are probably going to see the situation differently from the way an adult does and will behave differently. Although we know that it is good to talk about feelings rather than bottle them up, we think that you should be able to do that when it is best for you rather than when somebody else thinks that it is best for you.

And finally, we need (and appreciate) people around us who care even if we don't always act as we do. Because the first week is long and hard. Tina described it best when she said, "When you are alone in the first week, it wasn't like being alone. It was like not having the other parent when no one else was around. It felt like something big in my life was missing, and I felt very lost."

IT IS UP TO YOU

As we said, writing about the first week was hard, but it was important because we want to help kids get over it as easily as possible. There are many ways to do it. We have talked about our first weeks and some of the ways that we used to handle them. They might be good for you or they might not; you will have to be the judge of that.

We do think, though, that some of the getting past the first week will be up to you. You can make a choice to get over it easily or not. The kids we know who got over it quickly talked about it and maybe even wrote about it. The ones who had a harder time dwelt a lot on how bad everything was. Of course, you probably never felt this kind of emotion before, and it may be a shock that you will never forget.

But we think that you can look ahead. By the time six months has passed, everything may not be perfect, but you will have made it through the worst.

3

The First Six Months

When you get used to it you start smiling,
And your parent can see you gleaming,
Then you know all the hurt and pain is fading.

—Mindy, age fifteen.

CALMING DOWN

As you go through the first six months, you are more and more able to put the first week in a single-parent family behind you. As Noel said, "It's kind of like you want to step over the past and try to forget the worst part of what happened."

One reason you can is that you and the people around you are calming down. Life with one parent is becoming familiar. As Elizabeth said, "You are getting used to the sights and sounds of this way of living and are getting the feel of it."

The frustration of not being able to find answers and make some sense of what was happening is going or gone. Tom told us, "The main questions I had were about my dad. I guess I wanted to be reassured that he loved me, and I also wanted to know why he and my mom broke up. After six months, my mom was able to sit down with me and explain everything. She gave me a lot of moral support when I needed it most."

Many times questions get answered not just by talking about it but by people's actions and feelings. You become more aware of people and, whether they or you realize it, they are helping you sort out your questions and confusion. What helps, too, is the time that you spend wondering about your problems and the family. It is easy to get discouraged when you are doing all this wondering, but the truth is that time and thought heal wounds. If you keep at it, you eventually work it out, and you end up feeling better.

In many houses, the tension seems to be leaving, and the headaches that you had aren't there anymore. In families where parents have separated, there is not as much fighting as before. (You know, the throwing of deadly objects and screaming bloody murder.) The guilt is gone because your parents and other people have convinced you that it wasn't your fault. You are ready to start talking to people again and not be as quiet. As Laura said, "No more crying and all that gooky stuff."

When the tension and the headaches go, so does much of the confusion. Every family has a different way of handling it. Missy said that in her family, "It just went away. We got rid of it by not thinking about it." Tina said, "It ended for us, and there is no good explanation of where it went. But it was gone. We tried to get rid of it by thinking good things. We realized that we had to go on with life. We thought a lot about it. I realized that, no matter what I did or how I felt, my parents just weren't going to get back together. The only thing to do was make the best of it."

The nice thing that happens is that life seems to be getting organized at home. Most of the time, meals are back to normal (minus one person; you are *always* aware of that). Chores are getting done, and the house isn't such a mess. As Elizabeth said, "Things started evening out."

This starts to bring the whole family out of shock and closer together. Bronwen talked about her family: "There was a period after my mother died when we all went off in different directions. I was worried that the family wouldn't come back together, but it did." Everyone just seems more relaxed and at ease with each other. Elizabeth said, "The four of us (my mom, brother, sister, and me) became closer in that we did more things together (like go on vacations) and didn't quarrel as much." Or, if you are like many of us, you're fighting more. In other words, you're getting back to normal.

During the six months, friends and relatives start to accept the changes as well. Their sadness is gone, and they seem to be out of shock, too. They still offer support like money and caring but stop calling and writing as much. We think that they are more convinced that everything is okay.

A lot of us got closer to our grandparents in particular because they began to take care of us more. Noel said, "I would get home from school about two-thirty, I'd be alone until my gramp would get home at three-thirty, then my gram at four-thirty, and finally my mom at five." Darcey said, "I never really did have to stay home alone because my grandparents were always there. We lived with them, and it was like one big happy family."

Even so, school can be a struggle. Martha Rudd, principal of our junior high school, said, "In the first six months, kids from single-parent families often withdraw, and we notice a change in their behavior, in their grades, in needing a place to be quiet, and in having some emotions that they have to express." For Norman it meant getting into more fights even though his grades stayed the same. Bruce Bentley began to miss days of school, his grades went down, and his chance of making the basketball team was in jeopardy. Even so, most kids' grades do get better during the six months and teachers stop asking, "How are things at home?" Sometimes they get better because the tension is gone and kids can start concentrating again. Other times, as Pam Evans said, "My grades got better because studying was something to do to make me stop thinking about my parents."

It gets easier to talk to your friends, too. A lot of them know by now. At first they asked questions like:

Where is your mother or father?

Is your parent coming back?

Why doesn't your parent live at home anymore?

How did your parent die?

Do you miss your parent?

They wanted to know all the details. That was really rough. After a while, they stop asking questions and accept it. Actually, most of them sort of forget about it. And after thinking about nothing else, you are ready to forget it for a while, too.

A NEW IDEA OF FAMILY

You are starting to get a new idea of just what your family can be. This isn't something that you always plan. As Elizabeth said, "You just kind of grow into it."

The biggest change is that one parent at a time is now in charge of everything and has all the power to make daily decisions. You can start to realize some benefits from this change. For Tina, it meant "not having to worry about getting the runaround every time that I wanted to go somewhere. Let's say that I wanted to go to the movies. First, I'd ask my mom and she'd say, 'Ask your dad.' And then I'd ask him and he'd say, 'Ask your mom.' This could go on for like twenty minutes and finally I'd have to say to both of them, 'Just give me an answer, will you please?' "

When one parent takes over, we notice that kids are asked to participate in making family decisions. Elizabeth said, "We started talking over dinner or in the evening. We would all talk out problems together and make a decision that we could all agree on. For example, we had to learn to choose together the things that we could spend our time and money on. One time, we had to decide whether we wanted to buy a membership at the recreation center or a color television. We agreed on the recreation center because we thought that we could have more fun there than sitting in front of a TV. (Eventually we got the TV, too. My dad bought it for us.)"

Just because one parent at a time is now in charge doesn't mean that two parents aren't still affecting your life. If your parent died, the spirit of that parent can still be with the family. You might hear things like "Your father would be proud of you" or "Your mother would have wanted it that way." The parent you are living with may not want to let go of your dead parent for fear of letting that parent down. Also, it helps to keep the family together.

Most of the time a divorce in a family means your parents' relationship will change but not necessarily end. As long as there are kids in the family, your parents will have to have some kind of a relationship.

The best situation is when parents have stopped fighting because they realize each other's differences. Tina told us, "When six months had passed, my parents got along well, and I enjoyed that. I was relieved that they weren't fighting." Parents may even become friends. This is best because, as Julie B. said, "You can go on with your life and not worry about things like 'Mom said this' or 'Dad said that.'"

Too often it is just the opposite, and parents are still fighting over money and the kids as much as when they were home together. They may completely ignore each other and not even speak. This doesn't mean that they don't *need* to talk to each other. You just get forced into giving messages back and forth like "Tell your father that I want the support payment in the mail by Tuesday." They might be so mad at each other that they are still trying to hurt one another. We know a kid whose parent moved out of town to keep the other parent from seeing her.

Sometimes during this six months, custody of you isn't settled yet. Your parents can still be fighting over who gets you. This can make you feel happy to find out that both parents really do want you. Most of the time, it is a problem. Dorothy Ann Sweeney, a psychotherapist in our town with expertise in child and family development, said, "When parents battle over custody of their children, there is not only the loss of a parent but also complications for a kid." You may end up deciding where to live or with whom based on what will make everybody else happy instead of what you think would be best for you.

We were relieved to find out that most families don't get into custody battles over kids. According to Neil Moss, a lawyer in Bennington, Vermont, "Of all the divorces that I have seen, there are very few actual custody battles. After the initial disagreement, the husband and wife usually agree before they have that happen."

We think that kids going through the change to single-parent life feel that family is essential to them. Bruce, whose father died, said, "Losing my father made me realize that all family members, even those who are not close to me, are important."

The New Parent You Live with

Our parents were in better moods after six months. A lot of the scary and upsetting habits that they picked up, like being messy or unclean, biting nails, not eating, eating too much, drinking, or daydreaming, have either disappeared or are disappearing.

Instead of being grumpy or sad and walking around like a zombie, our parents seemed to be coming back to life. Darcey gave us a good example: "Mom was really depressed after my father died. By six months, she snapped out of it. She was like a kid again and fooled around with us." Terry Fiorenzo told us that her mother was okay after six months. "She was happy, and she could talk to me like a mother again instead of crying all the time." Noel said, "My mom just seemed happier. We did lots of things together. We went shopping, talked a lot, and laughed a lot."

After going through the hard times with the parent we stayed with, a lot of us saw our parent differently from the way we had before the change. One thing that we realized is that the parent we lived with was really a human being and wasn't capable of doing everything. As Margae said, "You find out that your parent has a side which isn't all-knowing."

This really becomes obvious when the parent you live with has to do all the disciplining. We think every parent has difficulty with it in the beginning, especially if it wasn't that parent's job in the family. Bruce said that after his father died his mother didn't provide as much discipline for his brother and sister. Roger, who lived with his mother after his parents divorced, said, "I could get away with a lot more from my mom. She just couldn't control me. If she tried, I would just not listen to her."

You also are finding out that one parent can't give attention to every kid in the family all the time. Bronwen said, "After all, the attention that gets demanded from your one parent is twice as much as now. Every kid in our family was saying, 'Dad, listen to me.' Sometimes it became a matter of yelling and screaming and sitting on the floor. Or my sister would thump around the house and mumble. Things would go crashing. Finally, my dad would say, 'Okay, Allison, what do you need?' "

The discovery that your parent can't do everything affects you in different ways. First, you are kind of shocked because you always thought of your parent as very powerful. Then, you might feel guilty because of the times that you didn't treat that parent like a human being. For example, there were times when you behaved badly or didn't give your parent time to be alone. Finally, you might feel relief that your parent is human and that you are more on the same level.

On the other hand, we also found out just how strong the parent we lived with could be. Each of us watched our parent take control of running the house and handling unfamiliar responsibilities. For example, some of us have mothers who had never worked outside the home before. Amyee said, "My mom really took charge of things. She got a job, and we started doing okay." A mother might also do maintenance around the house, like fixing a broken toilet, that most of the time a father would have done if he had been there. If you stay with your father, you are more likely to see him folding clothes, fixing the meals, and doing the shopping. Seeing parents make these changes can make you think, "Wow, things are really going to work out."

For many of us, the parents we stayed with became much more important to us. We began to realize that even though some of our other parents contribute to our care these parents would be the ones who we would be depending on. Missy said, "My mom became the person who gave us clothes, food, and a home to live in."

Some of us realized that this meant that we had better stay on our parents' good side because they had more power over us. Mostly, though, it meant for many of us that we got much closer to the parents we stayed with. (Of course, this isn't always true. Some kids we talked to didn't even want to live with the parents they were with.)

Your image of your parent can change because of what your parent is doing at six months, too. Many have started to develop new habits like:

Going on health food or cleanliness kicks
Changing hairstyles
Wearing different clothes
Going to work
Changing their jobs
Going back to school
Dating
Spending time with completely different kinds of people

Some are still struggling, but many, as Amyee said, "are starting to get excited about a new life." Noel felt this could happen because, by six months, "a lot of pressure was taken off their minds."

A New Relationship with the Parent You Don't Live with

Many kids are starting new relationships with parents who are out of the house. Some kids who didn't see their other parent for a long time are back in touch and experimenting with different ways of being together.

Our feelings for the parents who we didn't live with were

complicated. Sometimes our feelings grew. Tina told us, "When my parents first separated, I was upset. I was just getting to really know my father. It hurt for a long while, but then I realized that the splitting brought my father and me closer together than we had ever been before. I realized how much he means to me. That thought helped me to not get as upset. So in a way it was a good thing."

Most of the time a kid gets farther and farther away from the other parent. The greatest fear is that you might lose your feelings for each other. It gets harder to talk to the parent you aren't with on a day-to-day basis. You feel uncomfortable, maybe you are still mad about the breakup, and your parent is feeling guilty. Elizabeth said, "My dad and I went shopping and roller-skating and such. I felt like he was trying to make everything up to me. I think he had the feeling that if I got things from him, I would love him more. Not true; I loved him anyway." And, of course, you are feeling sad because of all this time that you haven't been together.

If your parents have separated, most likely after six months has passed it has been decided where you are going to permanently stay and what the visiting schedule will be. There are lots of different kinds of visiting arrangements. Some are really flexible. Chris and Matt live with their mother so that they can be closer to school and see their father whenever they want. And some are very rigid. Tanya has to be picked up and dropped off exactly on time every other weekend and for two weeks in the summer.

Your relationship with your parent will be affected by your visiting arrangement. The beginning is always awkward, especially if you haven't seen your parent for a while. Tom said, "My father lives thirty miles away, and, in the beginning, neither parent wanted to drive. It was kind of weird because I was getting used to not seeing him, and *pow!* I started seeing him again. After the visit was over, I had a real hard time saying goodbye."

Kids want everything to be the same, but it isn't. It can feel very hard to fit in. The new surroundings are often foreign, and you feel out of place. Your parent isn't the same, and there are always new people who affect your relationship with your parent. You can feel left out. This is especially true if the parent you are visiting is married or living with someone. You feel jealous of this person. Elizabeth said, "It was a little tense for me because I guess I felt intimidated by my father's girlfriend." It is even worse if your parent's new partner has children living with him or her. It can drive you crazy if you find *your* parent paying more attention to *someone else's* kids than to you.

If a parent moves out of the house and right into someone else's house, it can make you feel humiliated. One boy said, "Dad left, and three months later he was with my stepmother." One girl told us, "It makes you feel like he doesn't care about you or your mother."

During the first six months, you may begin to wonder if your relationship with the parent you don't live with is over. Amyee said, "My dad didn't call or anything so we just left it at that." Noel said, "I understood by then that I was being abandoned by my stepfather and his whole family. He was always calling or stopping in. He'd say, 'I'll take you out to eat Friday.' Things like that. He would always break his promises and make excuses. Finally, my mom told him to stop promising me things and to stay away. The broken promises were pretty upsetting so I was glad that she told him. I just kept it in and didn't say anything about it."

It is hard for a kid who has been abandoned by a parent to know what to do. We don't think that it would do any good to try to get in touch with that parent. If you do make contact, you may not be satisfied because you will always wonder if that parent ever would have called you. Of course, if you *really* want to try to contact your missing parent, go ahead. It is always possible that, as one girl said, "The missing parent may be afraid to make the first move and is waiting for the kid to get in touch." You just need to remember that it could be very easy to get your feelings hurt. The one thing we do know is that talking to people close to you about your feelings is important. It can really help.

If one of your parents died, you've maybe begun to realize he or she is gone for good. Until now maybe you didn't want to believe that your parent wasn't coming back. You would continue to imagine that parent walking in the door. Norman said, "My father used to be out a lot anyway, so when I would come home and not see him there, I thought he would be coming home soon." Some of us during the six months still weren't ready to accept our parents' deaths. If you feel the same way, we can understand why, but we think that eventually you will have to face the facts.

Almost all of us were still sad over how our lives with our absent parents had changed, over not being able to see those parents as much or at all, and over the realization that it wouldn't be quite the same again. We still thought (and in a way we always will) about what life would have been like. Missy, whose father died, said, "I feel mad thinking about it, and I feel sad in another way because I miss him a lot. I keep thinking things would be different if he were alive."

Dating Parent

Some parents don't date in the first six months. One reason is that they haven't met the right person yet. Another is that they may not want to create any additional confusion for the kids at this point. Or some parents just are just getting used to being independent and want to stay that way.

A lot of our parents did date during the first six months. We asked ourselves, "Why would our parents want to date?" We think it is a complex question and an important one because of the feelings that get raised.

There are many different reasons why parents start to date. Parents might date because they are lonely or bored or just because it is fun. They might date as a way of getting out of a depression. A lot of parents are still feeling sad or angry. They may still be feeling guilty.

Some parents start dating because they think they need somebody to take care of them. They may be struggling with being alone. This is probably a new way of living for them. They realize that they now have to take care of everything for the family, which can make them feel very lonely, scared, and serious. Or they may miss having the comfort of a family around them. Some parents feel that they don't have any friends, and dating is one way to start to make new friends. Elizabeth said, "I think my mom was restless, and she needed new faces." Sometimes parents date as a way of making absent parents jealous.

Some parents may even date each other again after being separated for a while. This can seem strange to a kid. Most kids are glad that their parents are trying to get back together. But you can be mad, too. Jenny said, "If you feel like one of your parents really hurt the family, it can make you mad that this parent is trying to get back in the family again." A lot of kids, especially those who are young, might not even know parents are dating because they didn't understand what happened in the first place.

Some parents date at bars, some at the movies, and some at home. Our parents dated all kinds of different people. One girl we interviewed said her father dated young, tall, skinny girls. One boy's father dated his coworker. Some parents go out with people who seem just the opposite of what the other parent was like. Ellen said, "My father liked to read so my mother started dating athletes." Some try to find people who are just like the parents who are absent. We also thought parents could become homosexuals and date people of their own sex.

The question popped into our heads, "What would parents date?" We thought that you might think this is a silly question, and you would either ignore it or automatically answer, *"People, of course!"* But we are serious. Naomi suggested, "Parents who have just started this way of living may have a hard time relating to other people so they might get close to a pet or really involved in a job. This could be a kind of relationship."

Some kids don't mind their parents dating and like what it can do for them. Dating can:

Get them out of their crabby moods

Help them to feel better about themselves

Encourage them to have fun

Stop bad habits

Make them happier parents

Almost all of us had pretty strong feelings about our parents when they started dating, even if we understood and thought it was a good idea. Some of us found it more difficult to watch the parent we live with start to date. Either your parent is leaving all the time or bringing people home whom you don't want to meet. At least when the parent we don't live with dated, we didn't know about it, and what you don't know about won't hurt you.

On the other hand, there are some of us who felt that it was harder to have the parent who was out of the house start to date. You are in the dark all the time. You don't know the person your parent is dating, and you don't know what is going on. You feel out of control. This makes it harder to get to know your parent's date and finally accept it.

We wondered, "Do kids show their feelings to their parents about the dating?" Mostly not right away. Some kids get mad and yell about it. We think lots of kids keep it inside because they aren't always quite sure what they are feeling or how they are supposed to handle it.

Your parent's dating can be a shock to you. Noel said, "When my mother met Bob, I felt angry, sad, jealous, and hateful. I was jealous because I felt that he was taking my mother away from me. (This sounds childish, but it isn't.) Everything started happening so fast. I know for a fact that it hurt me. I never thought of her having a boyfriend and, when I was finally happy about the divorce, her dating caused my feelings to change from happy to sad and confused."

In some way, we all feel abandoned when our parents date. You definitely are physically abandoned, but your biggest worry is that you are about to be emotionally abandoned. You start to worry that they are going to make their own lives and that you won't be included. Julie B. said, "I felt betrayal; I felt that my mother didn't need me anymore so she went out and found someone else."

You have just gotten used to living with one parent, perhaps that parent has begun to work, the other parent isn't as available to you or not available at all, and then you find yourself home alone one night or with a relative and you start to think, "Hey, wait a minute, remember me?"

We think that, when parents start to date, they do forget about the kids. Tanya said, "My mother started being really independent. She went out a lot. She felt that she owed it to herself for all the years she sat home taking care of us without much help from my father."

Kids can start acting very bad right about the time their parent starts to date. Sometimes you really try to torture the dates, especially if you know they are trying to get rid of you. Julie H. remembered, "One time I remember when my mom went out, I locked her and her date out of the house. My mom yelled, and he laughed. I ended up feeling much worse because I didn't get rid of the boyfriend and it just angered my mother." Molly Goldberg talked about when her mother first started dating. "She met a guy named Jim, and I hated him. When he showed up, my relationship with my mom changed. We grew apart a little, and I started being a pain. I was so mad that I kept everything inside, and I took it out on everyone. I started having a short temper, and I was a rotten person to get along with."

We think that kids behave badly because of all the fears they are having. One of the first fears you have is that your parent is going to get married right away. Questions you would like to ask your parent are:

Where does he or she live? (Is he going to live *here?*)
Is he or she married? (This is important to kids.)
Does he or she have kids?
Are you going to have kids with him or her?

Another fear is that someone is coming in to take the other parent's place. This can be a reason why you don't like one of your parent's dates. One girl told us, "I really don't know what he saw in her. Maybe I just couldn't quite accept her taking my mother's place." You aren't ready for that to happen in the first six months. In fact, you never really believe that someone can take your parent's place. You feel, too, that your parent is abandoning your other parent. Chris said, "I was mad. My mom was dating a nice guy, but I thought that he shouldn't be with her, my father should."

Sometimes one of our parents' dates tries to play the parent. When this happens, all of our feelings come unglued. Molly said, "Jim was always giving me lectures about my attitude, but I never listened. I didn't think that he had the right to tell me how to act or what to do. I was really cruel to my mom and him."

We aren't saying that every date is a bad person. Some dates are pretty good about coming into the family. Missy said, "I liked one of my mother's boyfriends. He was nice, and he did not try to make us leave the room."

These are some suggestions you might make to your parent when bringing home a date:

Expect kids to be uncomfortable

Don't leave us alone with the date unless we agree ahead of time

Don't be surprised if we are a little mad

Give kids time (longer than the first night) to be friends with the date

Sometimes dates are too eager for kids to like them right away. They might even bring presents with them. This makes us feel like they are trying to buy our friendship and ends up only making us madder. Kids just need a chance to get used to the idea of their parents dating.

Once you have a chance to get over the feelings, you usually realize that you are only *feeling* abandoned but really aren't. Once you understand this, you stop behaving so badly, too. Noel said, "I finally gave up being so angry because I realized that I was hurting my relationships with my friends and family. My friends were really sweet and put up with me, but I knew that I had to get better. I'll always remember it. Behaving badly doesn't always go away completely, though. Still, once in a while I get mad over nothing and take it out on my mother."

And you begin to understand that parents have their own needs. As Tina said, "I was a little mad at first, but I thought about it and realized my mom deserved to let herself go. It helped her because she found the right person. She is very happy and that makes me happy."

The best thing you can do if you are having a problem with your parents' dating is to talk to them about it (or let them read this book). Here are some thoughts that helped us:

It's okay
You don't have to like your parent's date
You don't have to not like your parent's date
Accept the person for who he or she is

Working Parent

A lot of our parents, after six months of being single parents, had to go to work for the first time, go back to work, or get a better job in order to support the family.

Watching a parent look for work can be scary. You wonder how you are going to make it if that parent doesn't find a job. Tina said, "When my mom was looking for work, I could tell by the expression on her face whether she had found work or not." We worry that parents might feel hurt if they don't get a job—like they weren't good enough. Most of our parents did find jobs. The biggest problem is getting a good job, one that is satisfying and pays enough.

A parent going back to work can be a hard adjustment for a kid. Parents often have to work at times when kids are usually home. As Tina told us, "When your parent is working, there is no one around to talk to. You can start to feel really lonely and down. You don't know what to do and who to turn to." It can mean having a babysitter for the first time or *being* a babysitter for the rest of the family.

When parents do go back to work, it is important for kids to know:

Where they work
What exactly they are doing
How to reach them by phone

You have to get used to "expecting the unexpected." All of a sudden your parent gets called to work right in the middle of a special occasion, like a birthday party or Christmas. Or you think that your parent is going to have a day off and then you find out that he or she has to go in to work. This makes you feel jealous because you want your parent home and mad for the same reason. Planning a vacation becomes a major job. You are all ready to go, then your parent's schedule changes and that is the end of that.

We wondered why a parent would choose to go to work rather than go on vacation. Mostly, we think our parents can't take the chance of losing a job. There are other reasons, too. For some parents, a vacation can be stressful so they choose to lose themselves in their work.

They also don't have as much time to be available for you when they are home. Jenny gave us a typical situation: "Let's say you show your parent a fifty-seven on a social studies test. Your parent says, 'That's okay, just do better next time.' You begin to get the feeling that he or she doesn't seem to be in the mood to help you and just seems too involved with getting everything done to take the time."

If your meals got better at home because everyone started

sitting down together again for dinner (very important for a kid), your parent's working full time can cause all that to end. When parents come home, they are exhausted and don't have the time to make a big meal.

When parents work, rules at home can get very strict. Usually, it is because they are tired and worried about us and don't have the energy to be as flexible as before. What is hard to remember when parents first go to work is that they are working because they love us and want to support us. Of course, we are glad that there is money to live on and that our parents are making sacrifices for us.

In the beginning of single-parent living, working parents try to take on everything: making money, cleaning the house, and fixing the meals. You can find yourself in a single-parent family with no new responsibilities. This may not seem awful. (Some of us thought it was great!)

We think that they might overdo it because they feel guilty about getting into a single-parent family. As Derek said, "It can be hard for a kid to understand when your parent is feeling very guilty. Sometimes you can repeat yourself hundreds of times before you are heard. Sometimes you never do get heard, and you give up. You get yelled at a lot, too, sometimes for the smallest things, like dropping a plate. The worst is when a parent keeps saying 'I'm sorry.' You appreciate it, but it ends up driving you crazy."

Or parents haven't learned that it is okay for a kid to have important jobs to do around the house. It is hard to convince a parent not to take everything on. Of course, kids don't always *want* to convince them. Some kids are still angry with their parents and don't want to do chores at all. Some just don't like the idea of extra work. Tina said, "I hate doing the dishes because my hands are in the water with all that gross food on the dishes. It makes me sick (seriously)!"

We found that it becomes important to help the parent out at home as much as possible while that parent works. We noticed that when the chores get spread between kids and parents, parents have more time for kids, and this feels better to us.

Taking on Responsibilities

For almost every kid we know, the change to living in a single-parent family meant taking on responsibilities. Our parents just had so much time, especially if they were working.

It isn't like we didn't have chores to do before. The difference during these past months is that now we are *really needed* to help out. It is no longer just a choice. There are times now when the family counts on you to do things like: cook, wash clothes, clean the house, and take care of younger brothers and sisters.

In a lot of ways you don't mind all the work that you are having to do. It can be new and exciting, and it's nice to be really needed. You learn to become more responsible and more aware of your surroundings. You find out how to respect other people's privacy and to fend for yourself.

We grew to like different parts of the responsibilities. Laura said, "I actually like doing the cooking. In the morning, I always do breakfast and sometimes supper at night. I love the cooking and feel self-accomplishment when I turn out a good meal."

You know, too, that your parents are starting over and need extra help. It makes you feel good to do more for your parents because it makes them feel better. Missy said, "My family didn't mind all the things they were doing because they knew that Mother was going through a hard time."

Many of the responsibilities you will be picking up will be ones that your absent parent used to do. Elizabeth said, "I had to start making breakfast. This was the time of day when we used to jump on my father's bed and get him to cook breakfast." Remembering good times when your parent did these chores can make you sad.

Older kids now start to be in charge when parents aren't there. Elizabeth told us about how you can go from being a kid to being a parent. "The first major job that I had was to take care of my brother, Chris, then ten years old, and my sister, who was eight. My mom went to work on the third shift and she wasn't home at night so I had to take on the responsibility of taking care of them. The first week or so that we did it was the hardest for me because they kept coming into my room in the middle of the night wanting something. In the morning, I had to start getting breakfast for my brother and sister and make sure they got dressed. Then, I would have to get myself dressed. I guess it was hard for them to adjust because they had to get used to obeying me."

If you are the kid in charge, it is easy for you to think that you are supposed to *become* the other parent and not just an older brother or sister. Bronwen said, "I really got caught up in trying to replace my mother. I tried to discipline my brother and sister. It didn't work out too well. Gradually, though, I got back to being an older sister."

In the beginning, when the family is changing, one kid might feel that he or she gets stuck with all the jobs. Laura said, "My dad started driving a truck, and he wasn't home when I needed him. I had to do all the cooking and all the housekeeping. My brothers (I have three of them) didn't do anything. It makes you feel like you want to give up, like your brothers don't care. But you don't because of how much help your father needs right now."

Parents often have a hard time getting schedules and chores set up fairly. In the beginning, one kid in a family will often get overloaded with responsibilities, and, if that kid is reliable, it is easy for parents to take advantage of the situation. This setup can cause bad feelings among kids in a family so it's important to be fair in spreading out the jobs.

Sometimes one kid will be most helpful for reasons we don't think are good. A kid might think: "Mom sure has been working hard. I haven't been doing enough around the house. I should work some more. If I do, maybe mom will feel better about herself, meet a man, and live happily ever after." We know that it just doesn't work that way.

Sometimes you get really mad about all you have to do. You think, "Why should we have to do this? If our parents had stayed together, we wouldn't have all this work!" Noel said, "First, I had to start helping with the dishes, then later, I had to take down clothes, feed the animals, and make the beds. I *hated* it. I would always think of some way to get out of it, and sometimes I did!"

Or you might think, as Bronwen did after her mother died, "If Mom can go ahead and die, then we can do what we want. I don't feel like making supper! I don't have to do the dishes! I'll just sit and read."

Some jobs you have to take on you might think are awful. Ellen told us: "I hate folding clothes and putting them away. It is so boring and time-consuming. I get exasperated at my mom for having me do it at all."

We think that kids should, instead of procrastinating, work diligently at helping out with things like taking out the garbage and doing the dishes. We think there are good reasons to help out, but we certainly can understand why kids might not want to help out or be angry about it.

Spending Time on Your Own

"One night my parent was out visiting friends. It was about ten o'clock, and I was watching this really scary movie. All of a sudden, the phone rang. It was my friend, and he told me he was coming over. Was I relieved!"—Tina, age fifteen.

One of the things that we had to get used to living in a single-parent family was spending more time by ourselves. Being alone can be very hard for a kid mainly because you are alone, not because you want to be but because you have no choice.

The worst part is getting scared when you are alone, and you can't get your mind off the situation. Jenny gave an example of the kind of thinking that can happen. "I am always imagining something that is not there. One time I was in the living room watching TV and there was a sock in the hallway and I thought it was a rat coming around the corner."

You wish most of the time that your parents would be there. Ellen said, "I had enough one day. I had had a terrible day. I had gotten yelled at for snapping at my brother and sister. I was so mad that I cried. There was no one to come up and comfort me."

You think, "Why can't they be with me?" Or you feel sorry for yourself and think, "My parent is raising me wrong." And, as Elizabeth says, "Then you go just the other way, and you think, 'They are pains, and I am glad that I am alone.'" Tina said, "Sometimes you really hate your parents for leaving you alone. It makes you feel like you are not wanted or needed."

When you are alone and don't want to be, writing down your feelings can be a way to spend the time. You can write letters to friends or relatives or just to yourself. Writing helps you to sort out your feelings, even if the writing isn't anything special or to anyone in particular.

Actually, during this six-month period, you find some advantages to spending the time by yourself. As Elizabeth said, "It was good for me. It helped me out. I wanted to be alone. I wanted the time to think and relax. The time I spent by myself I used to think about the divorce and get things situated in my mind."

Also, you aren't so restricted to doing things with the family as you used to be. You can have more choices over what to do with your time. It might mean new freedoms like being able to stay out later and having more control over where you go and when. The trick, though, is not to use the time stupidly. New freedoms can mean new problems. It can be very easy to get into trouble. Derek commented, "You might have a party, and your mom could come home when you least expect it."

We think that sometimes parents have every right to leave us alone. Tina said, "I was staying home alone more, but I understood why. My mom was going out. She needed a new life." It can be a chance for you to find a new life, too. There are places you can go and things you can do. You might get involved in activities that help you to make new friends. Friends are great and can make the difference in the way you feel.

STARTING OVER

By the end of six months in a single-parent family, life is basically starting over for both you and your parents. According to Dr. Stuart Freyer, a medical doctor interested in stress-related health problems who lives in our town, the first year in a single-parent family is stressful for everyone in the family because of all the changes. He said, "There are definitely more health problems. Studies show that adults and kids have more illnesses during this year."

Some kids are still hurt by the divorce or by a parent's dying or leaving. Some are feeling very mean and have changed their whole attitudes toward life. Even though you are out of shock, you still struggle. You might have liked your old life, and now you have to get used to a new way of life. You might feel changed because you had a set pattern and now that pattern is gone.

You are sad because the other parent won't be there to start a new life over with you and the rest of the family. What we mean is, as Darcey said, "you can now go out with your friends and their fathers and see them fooling around and not cry. But you still go home and sometimes cry because you think about it being that way for you. You wish that you could be fooling around with your father."

What hurts most is that starting over is going to affect your future. Debby said, "The shock went away after six months but not all the confusion. I still had a lot in my head. I didn't know how I wanted my life to be. I didn't know if I wanted a stepfather. I didn't know if I just wanted to live with my mother and brother. It was just so hard."

Starting over can make you feel fresh and hopeful because we believe you have the chance to fix old mistakes. You have learned and grown so much. As Tina said, "Basically, you have had to deal with just about as much as your parents. In a lot of ways, you are a new person. You can better handle being alone and being independent. You also start caring about yourself and other people. It was like you grew up in six months."

4

After a Few Years

REALIZING THAT YOU LIVE
IN A SINGLE-PARENT FAMILY

It can take a few years for some kids even to realize that they live in a single-parent family. This is because many kids were so young when their parents divorced or one of their parents died that they didn't know there was any other kind of family to live in. There are a lot of kids like this so we thought it would be important to talk about it.

If you are one of these kids, you probably began to gradually notice a difference between your family and some other families. We have two Julies in our group who helped to write this book. Both of them have lived in single-parent families since they were babies.

Julie H., who rarely has contact with her father, said, "I realized that something was different when I was five years old, and I would see fathers instead of mothers picking up their kids after school. I guess that my mother did tell me when I was younger. I really didn't have a reaction on the outside, but on the inside I was hurt and angry. I had the feeling that my dad didn't want me. I guess that I have outgrown that now, but I am not really sure."

Julie B. visits her father regularly. She told us: "I have been part of a single-parent family since I was one year old. My parents got a divorce, and ever since I have been living with my mother. My parents were having trouble for about a year before I was born.

Because my mom couldn't have any more children, they thought if they adopted a baby it might help their relationship. So they adopted me. They tried it for another year, but each of them was still miserable so they got a divorce. My brother and sister were older and knew what was going on, and it hurt them. But I grew up in a single-parent family so I guess that it's good that I never got really hurt."

As you can see, how you are affected when you realize depends on a lot of things, like:

How old you are

If you still are able to see your other parent

How much has been explained to you

We do think that many kids who have lived in single-parent families since they were very little see their families as Julie B. described: "I just grew up thinking that it was right to live with one parent and see the other parent on weekends. I just thought everything was normal."

YOU AND YOUR SINGLE PARENT

After living in a single-parent family for a number of years, you get to know the parent you live with very well. You know what certain expressions on your parent's face mean and what different tones of voice mean. You are more likely to do things with your parent that you wouldn't have done together if your other parent were there. Noel said, "We eat together, go for rides in the country, talk a lot, and laugh together." Amyee goes places with her parent, too. "I go shopping with my mom, we see movies together, and I even got her to go to the Journeys' concert with me."

Sometimes we think getting closer can be a problem if the parent gets closer as a way to "spoil" you because he/she feels sorry for you or fears making you mad. Or if the parent gets closer because he/she is afraid of being independent. However, most of us like the closeness, respect the parent we live with, and feel that parent is special.

A lot of single parents return that respect. A friend of Michelle's said, "The amazing thing about my parent is that she treats my sister and me like adults. She has always been like that. It makes me proud of her. One time my sister and I were home all alone, and we broke a plaque that was given to my mother by some friends who just got back from California. When my mom got home, we told her how it happened and how we tried to fix it and she didn't get mad." When a single parent is open-minded, understanding, and helpful, it makes you want to do more for your parent.

Because you become so close, you are more aware of how things are going for your single parent. And it becomes easier for both of you to share your feelings with each other. Elizabeth said, "I live with my mother, and we have become very, very close. It is nice because she is a friend and not just a mother." As a result, you learn to be more comforting to your parent and know the reasons why your parent needs it sometimes. This is important because kids often forget that life can be hard for parents as well as kids. One day, we all went home and asked our parent, "What are the hardest things about being a single parent?" We got a lot of different answers.

Norman's mother said, "No help in enforcing discipline; having to be both a mother and a father when it comes to school functions and sports events; and not having emotional support from another parent."

Missy's mom said, "It is lonesome for the parent; it is sad for me to watch the kids grow up without two parents; and it is hard to buy all the things the children want when there is not enough money."

Noel's mom said, "Worrying about not having enough time for Noel."

Amyee's mom said, "You try harder; you don't want people to say the reason the kids are like this or like that is that their parents are divorced; and you are more protective because the kids are all you have."

Elizabeth's mom said, "Trying not to feel guilty about supposedly denying your children the advantages of a full-time father."

Steve's mom said, "All the commitments."

Julie H.'s mother said, "Being totally responsible for the child, day and night."

Not many parents ever expected to become single parents. Being a single parent for a number of years can have a big effect on a person—sometimes for the better and sometimes for the worse. As Scott said, "A parent's personality can change: a crab can become nice or a nice parent can turn into a crab. Every situation is different." Regardless of which way a person changes, we have learned that single-parent living can be a more stressful life. The stress of it all is often why some parents decide to remarry.

But there are also a lot of parents who, after having made all the changes that go along with single-parent living, wouldn't want to go back to being a two-parent family—at least not while the kids are young. They want to avoid the conflicts that can go along with two-parent living. Some of the kids in our group who live in two-parent families came up with a list of things that are difficult about parents living together. These are conflicts that are less likely to show up in single-parent living. Some examples are:

Who:

Gets spending money?

Buys the kids clothes?

Supports the family?

Shops for the food?

Watches the kids the most?

Does the most work around the house?

Goes out and with whom?

How do we learn to:

Find time for ourselves?
Agree on rules and discipline?
Keep communications lines open?
Share our lives?
Live with each other's likes and dislikes?
Tolerate fighting with the ones we love?

Even though single parents are avoiding these conflicts, we know that sometimes they think, "Why do I live like this?" Julie B. said, "At these times, it is important to tell your parent that you understand and that it won't be so bad. We will make it. It helps to give your parent a hug. That always makes a parent feel good."

Of course, there are still things to be worked out in any single-parent family.

WHAT SEX IS THE PARENT YOU LIVE WITH?

Most of us live with our mothers, and a few of us live with our fathers. A lot of us live with our same-sex parent, but many of us live with our opposite-sex parent. We have found that this makes a difference in your life in a single-parent family.

Let's say you are a girl, and you live with your mom. This will mean that some problems will be avoided. We think that it is easier to go places together because you might (not always) have the same interests, like shopping, sports, or whatever. If your mom is single (and fun), you can even check out boys together.

We think the same is so if you are a boy living with your father. As Stephen said, "If your parent is a man, it can be easier because you might like some of the same stuff. You can talk to each other about personal things, like girls. You could go places together that you might not go with your mother. Most boys and their fathers like to go to ball games, watch the same kinds of television shows, or read the same kinds of books." And as Tom, who lives with his mother, said, "Living with your mother can be harder. Face it, you are just not interested in women's fashions. You are probably more interested in how last night's ball game turned out."

We think, too, that it can be easier to talk to your mom if you are a girl or your dad if you are a boy because you may understand each other better, having had similar experiences. As one girl said, "I can't talk about private things to Dad like I could with Mom. The conversation with my dad was always about football games and hockey."

You can be more likely to get help from your same-sex parent on picking out shoes or clothes. It can be difficult to try to explain current styles of clothes, what you are wearing, and why you are wearing it to the opposite-sex parent. It can be frustrating to try to convince your parent to let you wear a certain type of clothing, but we think that it is even harder if that parent is the opposite sex.

It is easy to feel left out if you have brothers or sisters who are the same sex as the parent you live with and you are the opposite. Because of their similar interests, they might have a tendency to spend more time together. If this happens, we think it is worth it to try to break in so that you don't feel so left out.

If you live with the opposite-sex parent, you may have trouble communicating. Talking about dates is difficult but maybe not as difficult as talking about other things, such as sex. You tend to feel embarrassed or awkward. We think that it is just easier to talk about the birds and the bees and how to handle yourself with the same-sex parent.

Talking about puberty can be uncomfortable. It is hard to go to your opposite-sex parent and ask questions. If you are a girl who lives with your father and you need your first bra, you probably are thinking, "I'm not about to ask my father to help me figure out what to do." Getting your first adult checkup is another situation that can be embarrassing.

Another problem that can come up when you live with the opposite-sex parent is that you can fall into taking the other parent's place. If you are a boy, you might feel you have to be (or sometimes want to be) the man of the house. Andy Shapiro, whose father died when he was twelve, said, "When I was thirteen, I was supposed to have the maturity of a man." If things aren't going right, you might feel it's your job to make them right. The same thing can happen to you if you are a girl and your mother is gone. As Margae said, "You may feel trapped inside an adult role that you can't, as a teenager, fulfill."

Of course, there are reasons why living with a parent of the opposite sex can be good. You can:

Learn how to cook

Share good times

Learn ways of living with a person of the opposite sex

And all problems don't automatically go away if you live with the same-sex parent. There are problems that can come up under those arrangements, too. For example, it can be easier to fight with the same-sex parent over things that you have in common. You might be more likely to get jealous of each other and of your material possessions, like new clothes. It can make you mad because the parent will be managing the money, and you don't have as much say over who gets what when.

It can be easier with a same-sex parent to get in each other's way. Your parent might want you to fit in his or her shoes. Or it can be just the opposite. You might hear, "When I was little, I was a little brat, and I don't want you to be the same way," or "When I was young, I married too soon, and I don't want that to happen to you." You can get so tired of hearing about it that you think, "I am going to do just what Mom doesn't want me to do to make her unhappy."

Making It Easier

Even though problems about sex make you uncomfortable when you live with your opposite-sex parent, there are things you can do. You can always ask your parent to help you with whatever you are struggling with. This can be hard, but it is a way to get things going and changing. Try to overcome the fear that your parent will laugh at you. Most parents will not. More than likely your parent will try to help you. It is worth it to start to try to trust your parent. Your parent has already had to go through everything that you might want to ask about.

If you are having a really hard time getting your opposite-sex parent to listen to what you need, keep explaining and maybe you will get through. Another way of getting that parent's attention is just to ask your opposite-sex parent to go out and buy you something that you will probably be embarrassed to ask for yourself. Then you will find out for sure whether or not your parent is paying attention.

If you are in your teens and need to see a doctor about personal matters, whether you are a boy or a girl, go ahead and do it. It would be a good idea to talk to your parent first. Don't let it pop up and become a surprise to your parent because you will end up feeling worse. Anyway, you will probably need to know things like whom to call, how to pay for the visit, and other things. If your parent doesn't pay attention to you or feels uncomfortable, you can always ask a friend or a relative you trust. Of course, if your other parent is available, you can always call for help.

You will have a lot of questions about sex as you grow up. You will have questions about your own body and that of your parent, too. This can (but doesn't have to) make you and your parent uncomfortable. Sexuality is all part of life. We think that if a kid asks a parent a question, the kid should expect an answer. And if you are a kid and feel uncomfortable about asking questions, just remember it's normal. If you want more information, there are books, friends, and other adults that you can use as resources.

INDEPENDENCE

After a few years in a single-parent family, we think that most kids are more independent than before getting into a single-parent family.

We think that a lot of kids in single-parent families become more independent because they have to be. There isn't much choice when one parent is out of the house and the other is working to get the money needed for food and bills. We think that, as Julie H. said, "A lot of kids have to grow up pretty quick."

Some kids do become independent by choice. As Darcey said, "By the time you are a teenager, you start to feel that your parents have done so much that you don't want them to do anymore." We think this is a normal part of growing up. But some just don't want to bother the parent because of how much pressure the parent is under.

Tina said, "The problem is that you may learn the wrong way of being independent from friends, like starting to drink at age thirteen. You may start to hang around with bad kids and get into drugs." Scott said, "One of my friends got caught with hard drugs. Nobody had told him it was wrong." This can happen when a kid just isn't ready to handle so much independence either because of not being mature enough or because the kid is still hurt and mad. One girl we talked to said, "I didn't want to stop being my mother's baby and everything."

Often, kids who live in single-parent families for a while can become more independent, and the parent and kid can become too busy for each other. This is especially true of teenagers, who naturally like to spend free time with friends. You end up not giving enough attention to your parent. Your parent fills up time by having more fun through spending time with friends or through extra work. Inadvertently, you don't pay enough attention to your parent, and then your parent doesn't pay enough attention to you. It turns into a vicious cycle. Usually, you end up feeling, as Noel said, "that your parent doesn't love you." Or your parent could think that you don't care.

When Independence Is a Bad Choice

Dependence is when you rely on someone. It is what makes any kind of emotional relationship between two people possible. The problem is that, as Elizabeth said, "All of your life you need to depend on other people. What happens is that you are always transferring people to be dependent upon. There may be a couple of years in your life that you don't think you depend on anybody, but even then you do. To a certain extent, depending on others is good. If everybody left, you would really be lost and just drift. But that doesn't happen very often."

One of the most common reasons that kids in single-parent families become more independent is that kids can be afraid to depend on anybody again. When a parent leaves for whatever reason, one word (Scott said it) describes how a kid feels: nowhere. From then on, until you learn differently, you imagine that everyone you get close to will leave you, and you will be back where you started. So you decide that being very independent is safer than being dependent.

Being this independent, though, can bring on different problems. Noel said, "You might shut people out, become bossy and selfish, because you may want to do things by yourself." Scott said, "If you get used to doing things your own way, you may be hard to get along with." And Tom said, "You would want to work alone all the time and not know how to work with other people."

This is scary to kids even if they are doing it on purpose. Darcey told us, "When you get to feeling too independent, withdrawing from everyone, and saying to yourself, 'I don't need anyone,' then you begin to worry that you will think this way forever, and you won't have any friends."

We know it is hard to let yourself get over fears of being "too dependent." We also think that it is good to maintain some independence so that, if someone who you heavily depend on stops being available to you, you won't feel totally lost.

But to stop depending on anybody is a bad choice. Scott came up with a game that we think could help kids who are having fears about dependence. It is called the Nowhere Game. It would be a game that you play by yourself or with other people. You would make a board with spaces on it. Starting at the bottom of the board, everytime you depend on someone else for anything and you have a good time, you move up a space. Learning to depend on others, we think, means that you are heading Somewhere.

E·ren though *you* probably didn't get yourself Nowhere, it is up to *you* to get yourself back Somewhere. This is the most important part of the game. You can depend on other people to help you get yourself out of Nowhere, but you have to be the one who makes the moves.

One part of the game that you won't like is getting hurt again. You definitely have feelings of self-doubt and want to give up. The thing is that you can't shut yourself off even if you might get hurt. The idea is to get up again and again, just like babies pulling themselves up in their cribs until they can stand on their own two feet. People who learn this part of the game almost always get Somewhere.

All Kids Feel Good About Some Independence

Basically, all kids like some independence. Darcey said, "I feel good about being independent because I feel a sense of accomplishment when I do something on my own. It makes me feel that I will be ready for life when I grow up." Just how much depends on the kid. Too much can be scary, as Margae said, for instance "when you find yourself in a situation where you are by yourself and you have to make a decision that concerns more than just you and there is no one to check it out with. That happened to me one day. I was washing some clothes. When I looked up, the soap was almost overflowing, and I was sure I was going to flood the house. I was really scared."

But not being given enough independence makes you feel like a baby. Of course, as Tom said, "How independent you become has a lot to do with the parent you are living with." As one of our parents said, "You can get overprotective because the kids are all you have." One girl in the group said, "My mom sometimes doesn't let me do things that my dad would if he were at home, like going to the store by myself. She is always afraid that I might get hurt." We can understand why a parent might feel this way, but a parent should understand the needs and wants of the children.

Independence usually means time to be alone. As Jenny suggested, "Time to yourself helps you to know who you really are and to figure out your problems." Or it can mean that you can be free to decide how you use your time. She continued, "Sometimes I study, or, if I want to, I just sit around and be bored. Bored tells me I don't have any work to do so it makes me feel good inside." Scott says, "Independence means you get away from your parents more often. I like being by myself or with one or two friends."

We think that kids who grow up in single-parent families learn to be resourceful. They like the feelings of self-sufficiency that come from being independent. Missy said, "I feel good because it will help me when I go out into the world by myself. It gets me ready for when I turn eighteen." Darcey included, "I feel good. I feel like I know what is out there waiting for me." Elizabeth added, "Through being alone, I have gotten more responsible. My mom trusts me more to stay home by myself."

You start to feel confident that you can handle difficult situations. Either you learn to believe that you can deal with your problems yourself or you learn how to find people to help you. Elizabeth told us about a situation that seemed hard for her at the time. "One time my mom went to the store in Albany. On the way, she ran out of gas on the highway. She called me (after she walked to a gas station), and she told me not to worry. I felt good because, even though I was worried, I kept calm." You even get to the point of wanting to take charge of situations. Norman said, "I would just rather do things myself. I figure that someone else is going to do it wrong."

Some kids who live in single-parent families are grateful for more independence after a few years. You begin to realize that some of the freedoms you have might not be there if the other parent were around. Missy said, "I stay out late and get to go to rollerskating. I wouldn't have been able to do these things if my father were here." We think that you generally get to do a lot more with your friends. The parent who is gone may have been much more strict than the parent you live with. And the parent you live with gets to know you better and trusts you at a younger age.

You realize after a while that you and your parent don't need to be together all the time. Although too much time alone is not good, it can get to the point where both of you are grateful for the time you have apart. It can help your relationship with your parent to have a certain amount of independence. And, believe it or not, you learn to find things to do.

Finding Things to Do

The most important things to struggle with when you have time to yourself is boredom and making smart use of the time. You may also get lonely, and being lonely is not a good feeling. It is important, but hard, not to feel sorry for yourself when you are alone. This will only make matters worse. The other thing, as you become more self-reliant, is to learn not to panic when faced with a new situation.

All of us have found ways over the years of filling our time and handling the loneliness. This doesn't mean that we always like it. Dora, a girl we interviewed who shares her time between her mother and father, said, "I still nag my parents sometimes. When I ask them to play with me, they say they are too tired. I get pretty tired of hearing it."

A lot of us, even though we still don't always like it, have become pretty creative with our time. We found out while we were writing this book that a lot of kids who live in single-parent families are good at filling their time. One day Michelle read in a school magazine about kids who live in single-parent families. It said, "Good News for Single-Parent Kids. Professor Thomas Yawkey at Penn State University has found that children of single-parent families tend to be more creative and imaginative than other children. They have more imaginary friends and play more creative games with their real friends. Yawkey attributes the difference to the fact that single-parent kids have more time to 'fill in' while Mom or Dad is unavailable—they tend to develop healthy imaginations to keep from being bored or lonely."

Dora told us what she does with her alone time. "I am trying not to nag my parents to play with me as much and am learning to play by myself. I know that I have developed more imagination since my parents divorced not only because I don't have as much time with them but also because there are not many kids in either place where my parents live. For example, I might go on a walk and pretend that I am going on a safari. Or while I am walking, I pretend that I have my own horses and I am riding."

It can take a real effort sometimes to find things to do. One boy said, "Whenever I get lonely and can't find something to do, I just get determined to keep busy." Many of us feel the same way.

Tina told us, "Whenever I am alone, I always think of the times when I am not alone. That helps me a lot." Cooking and eating can be fun, too. Another girl we talked to said, "Once, when I was alone, I made some chocolate chip cookies to help me feel better. It worked!" Elizabeth commented, "I listen to the radio or read a book." Jenny had a good idea: "One day I was sitting around doing nothing so I got some loose clothing on and started exercising. It was new. Afterward, I took a shower and felt refreshed." Margae suggests writing, doing puzzles, playing games, or doing chores. Noel said, "I call my friends to just talk or invite them over or write letters to my pen pals. I go to my gram's house, too, because they just live next door. I do a lot of different things."

Sometimes kids who live in single-parent families need to find things to do not only just because they are apart from parents but also because parents are involved with friends. Tina said, "Once, when a lot of people were at my house, I felt really lonely. They were all adults and talked about stuff that was either none of my business or something I didn't understand. The choices you have in a situation like that are to just sit there feeling lonely or go to your room and be just as lonely. I learned how to deal with it though, and I can make the loneliness go away or at least most of it. Now, when I get feeling this way, I talk to people close to me and try to spend a lot of time with them so that I am not so lonely."

Friends and relatives take on a new importance in your life when you try to fill your time. You find yourself wanting to get closer to other relatives so you will have someone to lean on when your parents are gone. You are also more likely to meet other kids with the same problems you are having. This really cuts down on the feelings of loneliness. Kids who have similar problems may want to help out because they may have gone through it before, or they know how you feel.

One of the nicest parts about being by yourself is that you get to do things on your own that you can't when other people, especially parents, are around. Margae said, "The last time I was alone I thought about a person I know; more or less I was really daydreaming. And it is a lot easier when you are alone because no one interrupts you!"

We have found that parents can also help us to not feel so bored or lonely. They help kids by letting them have dogs, cats, or other pets. And they provide things for kids to do like board games, puzzles, or home video sets. If you are having trouble with being alone, it can be worth it to talk to your parent about it.

Sometimes it's the small things that a parent does that can make a difference. Elizabeth said, "My mom works third shift, from 11 P.M. to 7 A.M. We have to leave for school at 7:50 A.M. so we get up at 6:30 A.M. to get our own breakfast and get dressed. When my mom comes home, she packs the lunches while she reminds us to brush our teeth and of what we are supposed to bring to school, then hurries us off."

RESPONSIBILITIES

We think that most kids in single-parent families learn to work hard. Peter MacMillan, a boy who lives with his mother and younger brother, said, "There is just a lot more to do. Mom works, and she has things she wants us to do. We are always trying to keep the house neat." During the school year, you are needed at home after school, and during the summer, there are more chores that keep you from going places.

These are typical chores that you have after a few years:

Mowing the yard
Taking out the trash
Doing the dishes
Making meals
Taking care of brothers and sisters
Doing the laundry
Feeding the animals

In the beginning, right after the separation or the death, you have a sense of excitement about the new responsibilities. That changes as time goes on. You do get used to it, but you also begin to resent the extra work.

We think that too often kids in single-parent families don't get enough time to play. When you are a kid, it is important to have free time. As Derek said, "If you have too many responsibilities, your life can become restricted. You might have to miss social situations or other kinds of invitations." Scott said, "You could miss time to play outside, do Scout stuff, and be a general nuisance." These are some other things we would rather be doing with our time:

Going to parties
Studying
Playing basketball
Playing baseball
Being with friends

Sometimes It Is Too Much Pressure

Margae and Jenny, who live in two-parent families, reminded us that it happens in their families, too. Margae said, "It seems that one of my parents is always telling me, 'Before you do this, you have to do that.' " We just think it is more likely to be a problem in a single-parent family. We think it is easy for the pressure placed on some kids to become too much. It can make them fearful of what will happen if they don't keep up. When a kid can't keep up, health can be affected both physically and mentally. You can become a very insecure person.

It is important to remember that, as Julie B. said, "Some kids can handle it and do just fine and some can't." Kids who can't handle it often react and don't talk about it. You feel like saying, "I am sick of the responsibility. I have to do something, like break a window." Some kids decide to run away. Other kids have to let their schoolwork suffer because of the other work that needs to get done at home. You can be so tired that you do your homework poorly or you don't do it at all. Then you can be so tired at school that your work deteriorates there.

You start to feel resentment for the parent who makes you do the work. You think that your parent piles work on you and that you aren't appreciated for it. For example, when you get home from school after a hard day, you feel mad if your parent says that you have to do a couple of loads of wash, clean your room, vacuum, etc. You need a break, and you don't get one.

Not everybody in single-parent families becomes overpressured from the responsibilities. You don't feel so much pressure:

If your family has enough money available
If you are an only child
If you are the youngest
If you are just a lazy kid

Also, some single parents, even if they work, manage the home in a way that keeps as much pressure off you as possible. A typical day for a kid in a single-parent family can sound just like a typical day in any family. Tina gave us an example: "Well, I get up and go to school. I'm in (boring) school all day, and after school I come home, clean my room, and eat supper. My sister and I take turns doing dishes. I do homework, take a shower, and go to bed."

Typical Fights

Kids' feelings about responsibilities depend on how they are handed out in the family. Brothers and sisters can have a lot of problems if the system isn't fair (in the kids' minds). The same thing can happen in two parent-families as well. But in single-parent families, where kids are likely to carry a bigger load, it can become more of a problem.

There are two kinds of typical fights that come about between brothers and sisters. The first one is, "Being the oldest stinks! Younger kids just get favored more." The other side of this problem sounds like "My older sister comes home and tells me to do this and do that. She is a pain."

Older kids are always mad because they feel that they have to do more of the work. And if you ask for help from a younger brother or sister, you often get, as Elizabeth said, "Yells and screams if it is not what they want to hear. Or if older kids divide up the house to clean, younger kids will clean and think their half is clean when really it is a big pile of junk. Then your parent comes home and helps *them* out." Worse yet, older kids often get blamed for work that younger kids didn't do even though it wasn't their responsibility. The other side is that younger kids think older kids are always bossing them around and acting like parents when they aren't.

A lot of times, older kids make the problem worse by doing all the work because it is easier than fighting with brothers and sisters or showing them how. One girl said, "If you try to teach a job, it can be frustrating. You don't know how to explain it, and the person you are trying to tell doesn't know what you are saying." And often, they don't want to know anyway.

The second argument is, "The girl usually has to do more. My brother never helps out." Or from a boy's side, "My sister sits in her room all day and pouts. I come home and clean the place."

There is truth on both sides. Naomi said, "In one family I know where the mother died, the girls had to take on all the responsibilities. The boys don't have to do anything." But then Derek said, "When my parents were divorced, my mom had to get a job. My brother was like a father. He told everyone what to do and did the cooking and the cleaning. My sister just did the dishes." We think that in some families girls have it easier and in other families boys have it easier. It all depends on the parents' attitudes.

Whether it is an older-younger fight or a boy-girl fight, the most important thing is that everyone has a share. As one girl said, "Sometimes one kid gets to be more independent than another. Kids get really jealous if one doesn't have to do as much. Brothers and sisters can end up as enemies." It is easy for brothers and sisters to feel hatred for one another. If kids can't solve these problems on their own, we think that parents should step in and help out.

Ways to Make It Work

There are things to do to make responsibilities more tolerable. Elizabeth had one idea: "First, my mom decided on the chores. I had to clean the bathroom, my brother had to vacuum, and my sister had to do the dusting. It was okay for a while, but then we got tired of doing the same job all the time. So we sat down and decided we would switch chores every six weeks. It worked out well. We also have other chores that don't switch."

One thing to remember, too, is that nobody likes to do chores. Stephen said, "I hardly do anything, and it feels like I do too much." Missy added, "I do the dishes, and I hate it. My brother takes out the garbage, and he hates it." We think things work out best in families like Amyee's: "In my family, everybody has a share. Nobody likes it, but they all know that it has to get done." Getting paid for some of the work helps. Noel said, "My mom does most of the work, but I make my own bed and feed the animals. I don't mind because I get paid, and I like to help out my mom." If you never have helped out before, you might get an unexpected reaction from your parent. Stephen said, "I would probably get some respect from my mom if I started helping." Norman worries: "My mother might have a coronary!"

After a few years, you can learn ways to schedule your time just as you learn to manage your money. Elizabeth said, "I have a system for combining housework and schoolwork. When I get home from school, I take off a half hour to relax. Then I do my homework while the information is still fresh in my mind. Afterward, I do my daily chores and the extra ones that I get from my mom."

If you are angry about your responsibilities, talking to your parent about your feelings can help to clear up problems. Elizabeth said, "I get mad because it seems that I have the most jobs, and I do the extra work. Half the time my brother and my sister don't do their chores and don't get yelled at as much as when I don't do them. I guess it's because I'm older. I complain to Mom, and she says I get extra money and other things when I need them so I shouldn't complain. She's right."

By doing so much, some of us have missed what we think would have been a more carefree life. But we also think that having had the responsibilities will help us in later life. We definitely all have a better understanding of what a parent goes through to keep a house together.

WHEN A KID BECOMES A PARENT
TO BROTHERS AND SISTERS

It's pretty common in a single-parent family for one of the kids to take on the job of being a parent to brothers and sisters. You usually grow into it gradually. It is most often an older kid but not always. It starts out with you being in charge when your parent is working, busy with other things, or around but in need of help. This means taking on the responsibility of having younger kids depend on you and look up to you for advice.

In the beginning, you are more willing. It makes you feel grown up and can also make you feel like a good Samaritan. If you are old enough, it is not uncomfortable to take it on. Bruce Bentley told us, "It didn't bother me so much becoming a parent figure. I was seventeen when my father died and was on my way to becoming an adult anyway. It wasn't like I was fourteen or fifteen."

After a while, though, you can get tired. You realize that having so much responsibility means time away from friends and other activities. The pressure can be too much for a kid, and it can hit you all at once. It can make you want to get away just so you can be alone and do one thing at a time. You find yourself blowing up at your brothers and sisters to have them get away from you. It can put a strain on your relationship with them. Elizabeth said, "My brother and sister and I fight a lot. I think we are just together too much." It can make the younger kids hate you. You have a tendency to get angry about the responsibility and take it out on the younger kids or your parent. When you get under pressure, you start finding fault with the parent who isn't home and blame him or her for the situation you are in. You might even start to think, "I don't want kids when I grow up!"

Some kids really need to get out from under the pressure but don't know how to do it. We think that some kids just say forget it. Maybe they don't say anything at all but get into trouble instead and use delinquency as a way to get out from under it all. Sometimes you just stop being so helpful.

It is harder to take care of brothers and sisters than someone else's kids. They are less likely to listen to your advice or pay attention to your authority. Because of this, you might end up bossing them around or being mean to them just to keep control. This can be hard on younger kids. Julie B. said, "My older sister was a pain when we were little. She would boss me around, then turn around and would want to do everything for me and treat me like a baby. She was a confusing kind of a parent." The responsibility can be scary, too. Elizabeth worries about it: "I always think, 'What would I do if there was a fire?' "

The pressure can be there not only from the responsibility but also because you begin to care so much. You start to look on younger brothers and sisters as your kids, and you start worrying about them. You even start lecturing them.

Kids who take on the job of a parent need certain things from the parent who asks it of them. Kids definitely need:

Trust
Extra freedoms
Independence
Understanding

The absolute worst thing that kids sometimes get is when a parent comes home from work, opens the door, and says, "What have you done? You haven't done anything!" If the kid is given a responsibility, then he/she really should have the responsibility. A parent shouldn't turn around and complain and undermine because the kid is probably doing the best he or she can. Getting paid by the parent can help, but we know that a decision like that should depend on the economics of the family.

We think that kids acting as parents could help themselves by encouraging independence in their brothers and sisters. For example, if your brother or sister had trouble at school, you should have him/her apologize to the teacher instead of your doing it for him/her. Older kids should also learn to speak up and say when they need a break rather than taking on more and more. It's good to remember that even brothers and sisters grow up.

We think that you do end up with feelings of accomplishment and pride when you can have the role of parent, be a help, and not be a pain. And when a parent tells you, "I couldn't have managed without you," it feels like it's all worth it.

MONEY AND SINGLE-PARENT FAMILIES

For most single-parent families, money becomes one of the biggest problems. Ms. Sweeney said, "I think that it is important to recognize that single-parent families are more likely to have less money." This is less often true for families headed by fathers because fathers usually make more money than mothers. A mother could have to go out and find a new job because she is not a housewife anymore. Bronwen said, "My mom had worked for a long time. She worked as long as she was able before she died. After she died, it became a struggle. My father's job didn't pay more just because she died."

Money isn't a problem in every family. It may be that your parents had plenty of money to go around so that, even after the divorce, your parent is able to support the family well. If your parent died and was able to afford insurance for the family, there might even be more money for the family than before the change to single-parent living. Bruce said that there were no money problems when his father died because his dad worked for the state and was well insured. Mr. Shapiro said, "We never had real financial problems after my father died. My father took care of everything. We just thought we had problems because we weren't getting richer after he died."

As a kid, you have to get used to the idea that the family may have to do with less. One thing that can make you sad is if money keeps you from being able to see your other parent as often as you would like. This can happen when your parents live far away from each other.

Sometimes you can't splurge on "unnecessary" things. Your allowance can get cut in half or completely dropped. Most special activities are limited. You aren't able to go out to eat or to the movies as much. You may not be able to get clothes whenever you want them. Margae said, "While all your friends have the latest forty-dollar jeans, you might not be able to because your mom says she has to pay a bill or something like that."

It Doesn't Do Any Good to Get Angry

It doesn't do any good to get angry. When you stop and think about it, you may not need new shoes as soon as you would like, or less expensive ones will do as well. You can still go to the arcade, maybe just not as often. If you start keeping closer track of your money, you can learn to manage it better and know when you can and when you can't splurge on something special.

In fact, nagging a parent for more money only makes matters worse. If the kid does get angry at the parent, it may turn into a long-lasting family quarrel. You have to understand that it is hard for your parent to cope with less money, too. It isn't your parent's fault that there isn't as much money. Your parent usually feels bad that he or she can't give you more.

We think that the best way to keep kids from getting angry is for parents to help kids understand the money situation. This won't make it all right, but it will most likely help kids calm down when they want something really expensive that they just can't afford. A good way to help kids understand is to have them get involved with the budget. That way they know where the money comes from and where it goes and how much things *really* cost. They will also learn how to budget for themselves when they are older. It can be helpful to let kids have a say in some decisions about where the money goes, as in where we should go on vacation this year, and have kids work toward saving for the trip, too.

Most Kids Are Willing to Help

Although we don't love the idea, kids are usually willing to help out with money once they understand. There are almost always places to find some kind of work. You can mow lawns, shovel snow, or possibly take on a paper route. If you are lucky, your school may have a program that allows you to go to school and work at the same time. The money you get could be for your spending money, or you could donate some of it to the family funds. In really bad situations, kids have decided to drop out of school to help support the family. We think that this is a bad choice. In the long run, it only hurts you and your family.

These are places to get jobs that wouldn't interfere with school:

Child care in private homes
Fast food restaurants
Stores
Farms
Motels
Hospitals
Newspapers

Even if you don't like the idea of working, it's better than stealing to get the things you need. In some families where money is a major problem, kids do end up stealing. The less money the family has, the greater the urge can be. This doesn't usually happen unless the family is really hard up. This kind of stealing is different from the kind of stealing that kids in single-parent families do to get attention.

The worst situation comes in families where a parent can't find work or loses a job. It's easy to get scared that there won't be enough money to go around. You think things like "Is Mom going to be able to take care of us? Where is the money going to come from?"

Kids need to know that when something like this happens, the government can be available to help out until the parent gets work or gets better. There are unemployment payments that people get when they are laid off from a job. Families can also get welfare payments, which helps to pay rent, and food stamps to help buy food.

Child Support: A Big Problem

One of the most important topics around money in a single-parent family is child support. It is usually paid by fathers to mothers because mothers have custody of the kids, and fathers are able to make more money. Michel Kimball, head of Child and Adult Services at United Counseling Service and a single parent, said, "Getting child support is important because it is part of a second salary to support a household."

There are almost always problems in single-parent families about support money. The most common problem is that the payments are late or not enough. It gets complicated for a kid. There are always excuses. Most often one parent tells the other parent, "I forgot," or "I don't have the money." And it is easy for a kid to get pulled into the battle. One parent might say, "Tell your father that I want the check on time," and the other, "Tell your mother she will get the check when I have the money." In these cases, you end up always being mad at someone. If, as a kid, you never had to think about child support, then you would have an easier adolescent life.

When a parent hears that a check is going to be late or less than the right amount, the usual response goes from mad to anger to fury. This usually fouls up your relationship with both parents. The parent the kid is staying with puts down the other parent. The kid then gets mad at both parents, the one who isn't paying the support and the one who is putting down the other parent. It's not good for a kid to feel mad at a parent for something that parents have done to each other.

The worst problem is when a parent who has to pay child support just disappears and the other parent never gets a cent. It makes a kid (and a parent) very mad. You can end up feeling like you aren't worth anything. It also is very unfair. We think that the only good reason not to pay child support is if the parent who is supposed to pay it doesn't have a job.

When a parent just stops paying child support, the question becomes, "How should the family get it?" The first thing to do is for the parent just to ask the other parent for it. If that parent ignores the request, the other parent can go to court. Mr. Moss said, "If you don't pay child support, you can be held in contempt of court. The parent could be sent to jail." This doesn't always happen, though. A lot of parents don't fight when they don't get their support because it is painful for everyone involved. It can be more trouble than it is worth. It is easy to spend a lot of money on legal fees and use up free time.

We think that a parent who isn't paying support shouldn't be able to see the children, at least not all the time. If a parent just doesn't have a job, that is one thing. But if the parent is choosing not to pay support, that parent isn't taking a real role in the kids' lives anyway. Of course, this has to be considered carefully.

It Can Affect Your Future

The hardest thing to accept about money problems is that it is going to affect your life. It can mean that kids from single-parent families, as Ms. Sweeney told us, "may have fewer choices. It can cause kids to drop out of school. If the family has a comfortable amount of money, kids can think freely about going to college. If they don't, it may be very difficult." This can make you feel angry and depressed. We think that it is important for kids to start planning their education early so that they can prepare for it by working harder in school to get a scholarship or a grant. You could probably check with counselors in your school for more information about choices.

MORE ON DATING

Some parents never date after they become single parents. Mr. Shapiro said, "My mom never dated, out of respect for the kids. There was also the stigma of a stepfamily. My fantasy was that she was worried about us. But she was very shy at forty-five. She came from a traditional Jewish family. You live for the man when he is alive and for his memory after he died." Some date for a while and then stop for the same reasons that Andy's mother didn't date. Nowadays, most parents date after being single parents for a few years.

Parents' dating is a problem for most kids no matter how long you have been in a single-parent family. It isn't the same as when your parent first started dating, but most of the time, you have feelings to work out about the dating. We don't think it makes much of a difference whether your parents are divorced or whether a parent has died.

You always want to feel more important to your parent than a date. This may seem selfish, but it means a lot to kids. Christie Becker, a girl who lives in our town, told us, "It makes me feel good to know that, if I ever have a special performance at school, my mother would be there and not go out on a date."

This doesn't mean that kids always hate their parents' dates. Sometimes you really like them, become good friends with them, and get upset if your parent stops going out with them. Christie continued, "My mom dated this guy for two years, and then they stopped dating. I don't know why. I am still friends with his daughter. He was nice. I liked him."

One thing about living in a single-parent family with a dating parent is that kids are more aware of sexuality. We talked about parents who became homosexuals. This was hard for us to understand. We think that kids with homosexual single parents would have a lot of trouble adjusting to it. Kids might feel uncomfortable and worry that they will become homosexual as well. If it is too uncomfortable, kids might not want to live with the parent. We know kids who do live in this type of family and don't think that they will automatically become homosexuals because of it. We are sure that it would be a worry for a kid and may take some special effort on the part of the kid and the parent to adjust. If you are a kid who worries about it, you can always get some counseling to help you understand your parent and yourself.

An Uncomfortable Part of Dating

Sleeping over can be an uncomfortable part of dating for the kids and the parent, and so we think it is worth talking about. If you are little when your parent starts dating, you usually think the date is only a friend. It may just be something you think and not even something a parent says. This may be the reason that one day you like a date and the next day not. Something happens and you think that this person is going to take the other parent's place. Oftentimes, the thing that happens to make the kid realize that a date is more than a friend is the first night that the date sleeps over.

Kids do have opinions about their single parents and dating. A lot of kids would feel better if parents dated for a while before they begin to sleep over at each other's house. Also, kids don't like it if they find out that their parents' dates are married. It just seems lousy. The married date might turn out to be one of your friends' parents. If the friend finds out, it could be taken out on you.

One of the ways that we discussed this part of the book was to put on a play about life in single-parent families and then talk about the play. It always helped us to sort out our feelings about the topic. This was one of our favorite activities, and we thought that you would like to see the play we did on a date sleeping over. We made up a family named the Dingledorfs, who were the stars of every play. This play is called *Ms. Dingledorf Goes to the Disco.*

The characters are:

Ms. Dingledorf
Ms. Dingledorf's date
Amyee Dingledorf (fourteen-year-old daughter)
Darcey Cockledoo (friend of Amyee)
Scott Dingledorf (three-year-old son)

First Scene: Morning at the Dingledorf home.

Ms. Dingledorf: Wake up. It's time for school.

Dingledorf Kids: What's for breakfast?

Ms. Dingledorf: Eggs and toast. I have a busy schedule today. I might have to work late. There are some business people coming to town, and I might have to take one of them out. But I will be home to make dinner for you.

Kids: Okay, Mom.

Second Scene: Home for dinner.

Ms. Dingledorf: Would you kids like burgers and fries? I'm going out to the disco with a guy from work. We'll be back at one.

Kids: Great. See you at one. (While Ms. Dingledorf is gone, Amyee and Darcey have a party.)

Third Scene: Home from the Disco.

Ms. Dingledorf: Okay, girls, it's time for bed. (Girls ignore her, so she puts Scott to bed and comes back.)

Ms. Dingledorf: Okay, now it is time for bed.

Amyee Dingledorf: I think we will stay up until your date leaves.

Ms. Dingledorf: That will be too late, we are going to have some coffee.

Amyee and Darcey: Great, we will have some coffee, too!

Ms. Dingledorf: No, we want to do some talking over coffee.

Amyee and Darcey: Good, we feel like talking, too!

Ms. Dingledorf: I give up. Let's call it a night. (Amy and Darcey offer to walk the date to the door.)

Amyee and Darcey: It's time for you to leave. She had a nice evening. Maybe she would like to do it again some time, thanks.

Ms. Dingledorf: (Getting angry.) Amyee, I can handle my own life!

Amyee: You were going to have him stay over night!

Ms. Dingledorf: I was not! Now, go to bed!

Amyee: Are you going to see him again?

Ms. Dingledorf: I might, but it is none of your business.

The End.

We came to a lot of conclusions after we did a play about a date sleeping over. The most important one is that, even though in the play the kids were trying to tell their mother what to do, we really think that kids shouldn't interfere with their parents' lives (even if you want to). We basically agree with Christie, who said, "My mom doesn't ask me what I think about her dates, and I don't really care. It's her life, and she should make her own decisions. If I didn't like him, I *might* ask her to not bring him to the house, but I wouldn't ask her not to see him." It is pretty natural, though, to want that date to fit your specifications. It isn't really fair, but you do it.

We know that a single parent needs somebody else besides the kids. You may always have some feelings about your parent and a date; that's natural. But if you want to confront a parent with your feelings, we think it should be done after the date has left. Imagine if your mom told you that she didn't approve of one of your friends while the friend was at your house. You wouldn't like it.

Another thing that we found out doing the play was that we would have a lot less trouble with a parent having a sleep-over date when we weren't going to have one of our friends at the house.

Kids are sometimes afraid to bring friends home because they might be embarrassed. We always imagine things that it might be one of our friends' parents or that our friends would go to school the next day and talk about us. If kids and parents discuss it, we think it will go a lot better.

Not only kids but parents, too, act embarrassed or ashamed when they first have dates stay over. Julie B. said, "Once you become a teenager and have some understanding of sex, you know what is going on." One girl said, "I remember when my father dated and the date came to stay overnight. I asked my dad, "Why did you hide this from me?" You appreciate it if they talk to you about it, at least ask if you mind. It can feel bad if your mom or dad doesn't warn you about it, and you find out the next day or that night. You aren't shocked; it is just awkward. It helps, too, if a date who has stayed overnight stays and talks to the kids a little bit in the morning. That way kids just feel more at ease and safe.

Something we found out that surprised us is kids have different standards for men and women. We don't think it is fair, but it happens. Let's say that a man brings a different woman home every night. It would bother kids (different dates every night drives kids crazy whether they sleep over or not), but not as much as if a woman brought a different date home every night. Men have no image problems if they date a lot of different people. Women are thought of as sleazy or prostitutes if they do the same thing. For some reason, society has put these values on men and women.

WHEN THINGS DON'T WORK OUT

Every kid in every single-parent family isn't always close to every single parent. From what we have described, you can see that there are many things that might not work out, and some single-parent families don't ever learn how to live together. Sometimes a kid and parent don't ever get over the other parent not being there. Or a kid and parent just don't like each other.

All families have fights over things like money, boyfriends, girlfriends, and school. But with the extra stress that can go along with single-parent living, the fighting can get worse and hurt the family. One boy told us, "I guess we have just grown apart. Half of the fighting is my fault, I beat on my little brother. Half is my mom's, too, for yelling at us for things we didn't do. I try to avoid the fights, but if they get started, I jump in." Sometimes kids who live with just one parent fight with that parent more. They often know that they can hassle a parent who doesn't have the energy to fight back. It can be easy to take advantage of a parent when you know you are in a better negotiating position. When this happens, tired parents give up.

Another reason that things break down is that sometimes a parent will get so protective, even after a few years, that you won't be allowed to go anyplace. One girl said, "It drives me crazy because I go out with a friend, and my mom makes me call every hour." The problem with this in the long run is that you might not become a totally independent adult. In the short run, it makes you want to fight for freedoms that you think other kids have and you don't. This can cause a lot of tension at home and make you want to leave. Or you can start to bounce back and forth between parents' houses because things don't quite work in either house. This makes you feel depressed and downgraded.

It is definitely hard on everyone when a home starts to break down. But kids in single-parent families can go other places to live. Some might go to aunts, uncles, foster homes, or close friends. This can happen when the other parent isn't available at all, when a kid doesn't want to live at home anymore, and when the parent doesn't want that kid there either.

But we found that it isn't always bad for everyone. We interviewed a boy named Roger who left his mother's house to become adopted because things were going so badly. He said, "My parents broke up when I was nine years old. I was living with my mom after that. I wasn't doing well. I hated school and was ready to quit. I was getting older and didn't have anything to do. Most of the time I spent hanging out on the street. It was at about then that I met Doug Sorenson at the recreation center. I was fourteen years old.

We started spending time together and doing things together. Eventually, we got much closer. One day he asked me if I wanted to be adopted. I talked to my family about it a lot. My sister had a hard time with it, but my mom thought it was a good idea. I ended up getting a lot of support from them.

"Doug really helped me. There had been no one to push me before. I really don't think the school could have done anything else. I have to give all the credit to him. In the beginning, I called him Doug. I realized that he cared so much about me that I wanted to think of him as my father. My father stopped coming around after my parents divorced. So I started calling him Dad. In the beginning it was hard, but I thought that I would never find anyone like him so it fit. I even decided to change my name.

"It is funny, but when my mom and I were living together, she could never show me love. Now she listens to me and understands me. It's good. I guess, if you're a kid who is having a hard time in a single-parent family, going to live somewhere with someone who can help you is worth it."

Everybody doesn't end up as lucky as Roger. Some families never split up entirely, and some kids never stop getting bounced back and forth. We just think it is important for kids to know that if things are going very badly (this can be true in two-parent families also), it doesn't *have* to be the end of the world.

LIFE WITH AND WITHOUT THE OTHER PARENT

Ellen said, "The biggest difference for me living in a single-parent family for the past few years is my relationship with the other parent. I don't feel like I need him anymore." One girl Michelle interviewed said, "After a few years (she had been in a single-parent family since she was two), I realized that, even though I lived with only one parent, my other parent still loved me."

These are two different kinds of experiences that kids can have when it comes to their relationship with their other parents. We think that, regardless of how good or bad a kid's relationship is with the out-of-house parent, it takes more work to maintain and is more easily damaged.

What can most likely put a dangerous hole in your relationship is not having enough time with the other parent. You just aren't as available to talk to each other. Your communication with that parent can be limited. Julie B. said, "I can ask my mother for things that I can't ask my father for. It's like I'm shy with my father. I think that if my parents had not divorced, I would have been much closer to my father than I am. I never had the chance to live with him."

You can feel distant from your parent even if that parent loves you and you really love her or him. For example, let's say your parent calls and says that getting together isn't possible right now. You both feel uncomfortable, and then you feel as though the caring isn't there anymore. It's easy to resent or be angry at your parent for not making the time. You really do need to be with your parent. If your parent doesn't at least try to see you, it could hurt you.

It can just get too easy to get to the point where, as one girl said, "I feel like we are breaking off. We had a falling-out, and I avoid him. It's scary." You see that parent differently, too—less like a parent and more like another grown-up. That can be okay sometimes, but it can make it easier to see your parent's faults. Things you would have overlooked now stick out. We think this is because we are getting older, but part of it goes along with single-parent living."

A common thing that can happen is that you don't realize your parent is changing. It can be when a parent moves in with another family, gets married, or has a live-in mate. And your parent doesn't realize that you are changing. Julie B. said, "I think that parents you don't live with have a hard time realizing that you are growing up. For instance, when I go to visit my father, I might want to walk down to the corner store for something. He will say that I can't go. I think that he is trying to overprotect me." Elizabeth said, "My father treats me like a baby. He wants to keep me in Polly Flinders dresses."

It isn't unusual that, after a few years, kids and parents start to get to know each other. Julie B. told us about her experience: "Last summer, I spent three weeks with my father. We started discussing personal things. I think it wasn't me as much as it was him. We talked about the divorce. I wondered whether or not he still cared about my mother and regretted breaking up. We just talked and talked. He did the same thing with my brother. He opened up his feelings in a way that he had never done before. A lot of things that I didn't know about him I found out. Before this summer, I had given up the idea of getting to know him."

Although you accept it by now, you never really get over the feeling that the parent who is away should be living with you. You are afraid that your parent won't be there one day when you need that parent most and may be gone forever.

VISITING

In the beginning, visiting your other parent feels awkward. After a few years, the awkwardness goes away. You accept the idea that this is how it is going to be and do the best you can with it. There can be some really positive parts about visiting.

Dora, whose parents share custody of her, said, "It is nice because it is different going to two houses. My dad's place is very small, hardly big enough for both of us. There is no running water and no bathroom, and we live on the tip of a big hill. But it is quiet, and we can spend lots of time talking to each other. We listen to different kinds of music and listen to the radio more." You won't get as bored in one home seeing the same scenery all the time. A change is good once in a while.

It can be fun to visit because you get stuff from the other parent that you don't from the parent you live with. You can have more friends because you can make friends at both places. If the parent you are visiting has remarried and there are kids in the family, it can be like having new brothers and sisters. They can even become good friends. And, if your parents like each other, it can be fun to talk with them about visits. Ms. Kimball said, "The kids' father and I are really good friends. I like his wife and him a lot. They come down to the house, and we all have dinner together. We go to all of the children's activities in school together. That may be different from the usual situation, but it really works for the kids."

Visiting Has Its Tricky Parts

Visiting has its tricky parts, though, that can get tiresome to a kid. Going back and forth between houses can be exhausting after a while. You are usually forgetting things at one place or another. Dora said, "It seems like I was always leaving something. One time I remember in particular, my marking pens were at my mom's, and my paper was at my dad's. I remember yelling, 'What is the point?' Then we came up with the idea to make a list of things that I needed and keep a set at both places."

Commuting can get to be a hassle. Long rides in particular get boring. You want to visit, but you don't want to spend an hour in the car. Sometimes the parent that is supposed to pick you up will be late, and you start to worry that the parent just isn't coming.

It can be hard going to a new environment. There are usually problems that come up about changing rules. What you are allowed to do at home may not be allowed at the other parent's house. Kids don't want to get into trouble, but sometimes it just can't be helped. One thing that really helps is to get the parent to lay down some solid rules just so you can have a good time.

If you and one of your parents live in the country and the other parent lives in the city, it is a big change. It can feel scary and unfamiliar no matter which way you are going. You are much more restricted in the city, and you really have to pay attention to what your parent says because your parent will have your best interests in mind.

Once you do get there, you might not have enough to do. When visits are first starting, everybody seems to make a special effort. But as they go on, both you and your parent can start to take each other for granted. Sometimes the parent you are visiting won't want to do things with you. It can get pretty boring doing nothing but watching TV. Tom said, "I like to drop little hints like 'I wonder what's going on at the park' or 'I feel like a game of Pac-Man.' " Sometimes this gets the parent mad, but it can work. Just make sure you know what kind of mood your parent is in. If you don't, it could mean trouble.

It really makes a kid mad when visiting is set up every few weeks or so, and the parent goes out on a date on one of the two nights that you are there. It just seems that, if that parent had all the time in between visits alone, it would be possible to spend the time with the kids while they were there.

Partly, finding things to do with each other can be hard because your habits change and your parent's habits change. A parent and kid may visit a lot in the beginning. Then you start to skip visits and have lives of your own that don't mix much. Sometimes you don't feel like you know each other anymore. You might not even be able to fight about it because the closeness will be gone, and you won't know what to say. When parents move far away from each other or if the parent you are visiting has remarried, you may only see your parent once a year, if that much. It is easy to get angry and resentful and begin to hate the parent.

If this happens, we think it is important for kids and parents to try harder to get to know each other again. Things can get so bad sometimes that parents and kids just stop wanting to be with each other. Making the effort could avoid bigger problems later on. The best way to get started is just to talk to the parent about how you are feeling. Maybe you can arrange to talk to each other more often on the phone or write notes to each other about what you are doing with your time.

It can take some time to figure out the best amount of time to visit. Dora said, "In the beginning, it was two days here and two days there. I was always packing and never had time to settle. I was always trying to divide a week equally, and that is impossible! Then,

I went to one week here and one week there and it was much better."

One thing that affects your thinking about visiting is you may feel guilty about leaving the home where your parent is all alone. It is really important for a kid to remember, as Dora told us, that "If you are going back and forth between parents, you don't have to make it equal." You could feel you aren't spending enough time with the parent you are visiting. If you do feel this way, you might not want to leave. You could fear that you will hurt one parent's feelings if you go, but you might hurt the other's if you don't go. You should talk to your parents because maybe you don't need to feel this way.

Some parents try to bribe kids to stay longer or to even live with them. This only makes the kid feel more guilty. Kids are almost always sad after a visit and feeling a little insecure anyway, and that is enough.

Making Visiting Easier

We think there are things that parents and kids can do to make visiting easier for everybody.

Kids can:

Work at not just sitting around and being bored
Discuss what they need with the parent
Figure out the best visiting schedule for them
Help out when they visit to make extra time
Not bug a parent or make the parent feel guilty
Try to understand parents' feelings and not just their own

Parents can:

Work on not discussing the bad times in the family
Make an effort to do things with kids while they are there

Date when the kids are not visiting

Have kids help make visiting arrangements

Help to make the transitions smooth

Not fight around visiting time

Never force a kid to visit; it doesn't work

Make sure kids know when they are going to get picked up and taken home

The last thought we have about visiting is for kids to remind parents, if they are feeling nervous that kids are not having fun, not to overworry (even if you are complaining). Sometimes parents will try to *make* you have fun because they are afraid you won't like them. Let parents know when they are trying too hard. Tell your parent that you came to be with him/her.

CAUGHT IN THE MIDDLE?

"My mom and dad are not friends and I am always in the middle. I try to avoid it, but it's hard. My mom talks to me and not to my dad, and my dad talks to me and not to my mom. I say, 'Just talk to her or him,' and they say, 'We can't.' It usually happens on weekends when I visit the other house. (My sister lives with my mother, and I live with my father.) It is the same for my sister, too. I would like to know why they can't get along even after they have been divorced. Occasionally, we have serious talks about it. It always ends up with my dad giving his side and my mom giving her side. I think that if I could suggest one thing to make living with single parents better, I would tell parents to communicate directly, not to go through their kids." This is what Sam Stempf who lives with his father, had to say when we interviewed him about living in a single-parent family.

Even a long time after a divorce, this can happen. A lot of parents just really don't ever learn to like each other. One girl we know said, "My parents don't speak to each other at all since they broke up." Another kid told us, "My parents just hate each other." With some parents, it can go back and forth. At six months they get along great, in a year they can't even stand the sight of each other, or vice versa. Elizabeth said, "For a long time, it was nice. Things worked well when they didn't get in each other's way. We were able to see Dad whenever he wanted. Now they don't get along as well." This is still one of the hardest things for kids to handle. You may have to face the fact that some parents never have worked it out and never will.

The worst situation for a kid to handle is when one parent talks about the other parent. It gets you mad because you are torn. One parent gets after you about the other parent and says something like "You should be living with me. Mom is a rotten parent." If this happens to you, we think the best way to respond is by saying nothing in order to avoid starting a fight between your parents.

A lot of parents do realize their mistakes after a few years and decide to get along some way, if only for the sake of the kids. Kids get scared when their parents don't like each other, even after a divorce or death. Laura told us how some people she knows stopped fighting. "Once in my uncle's house, he and his girlfriend were fighting and the kids were crying. All of a sudden they stopped fighting, and one said, 'Honey, look at these kids.' So they sat down with the kids and told them it was not the kids' fault, and the reason that they were fighting was because adults sometimes have problems of their own."

Sometimes parents get sick of fighting not only because of the kids but also because they get tired of hurting each other. One girl told us, "Every time my mother and father fought, they would end up crying and not speaking to each other because they would always say something that they didn't mean. Finally, they decided they would both be better off just not fighting."

Some parents are able to accept each other as friends after a while. Tina said, "My parents are pretty good friends. My mom has learned to not hate my father like she used to." Another girl told us, "My mom and dad talk out problems now and tell each other why they feel whatever way they feel."

It is much better if parents can manage to get along so that kids don't have to always choose sides. We think that when parents get along, kids are likely to see both of their parents more often. One girl said, "I know the reason my mother doesn't come to see me is that she just wants to avoid my father."

MISSING PARENT

It is always going to be hard to cope with the fact that a parent is missing.

As Margae said, "It isn't like getting a bad report card. You can't just snap out of it." A lot of people in your life will not understand how you feel. Even most of our parents will not have gone through what we have experienced.

Kids always think that they have missed so much without the parent. Missy said, "I missed my dad being around, but most of all I missed someone to call my real father." Norman added, "The things I missed most about my dad are his not being around, not going places with him, and not seeing him." If you never even met your parent, it is easy to feel, as Noel does, "I was deprived of what was really mine."

Some kids have a parent, but the parent doesn't care much about the kid. We think that it is much harder to have a parent who doesn't care about you than to have a parent who has died. The missing parent just lives a life without the kid. When a parent does that, the kid feels so rejected. You have to live your whole life knowing that your parent doesn't care for you. If your parent has abandoned you, you resent that parent for walking out. For example, you may come home to an empty house one night, you feel like no one is there for you, you begin to miss your other parent, and then you hate that parent. You might think, as Stephen did, "If my father couldn't handle it, why did he have me in the first place?"

Amyee said, "I hate him and think he is cruel not to pay child support or even call, write, or send presents for holidays."

The thought is always there that life would have been different and better. Debby said, "If my father had not died, I wouldn't have all the problems that I have now, like waking up in the middle of the night and crying. I sometimes cry so hard because I just want my father to be here. I think we would have done a lot of things together. We would go sliding in the wintertime or out to supper. I think we would be just like other kids with their fathers. Other kids look so happy with their fathers, and they talk about all the fun times they have and all the places they go."

We think it can be hard on you if you have grown up with this feeling. A lot of times the feeling grows as you grow. Even after a few years, you can still feel like you don't want to go on anymore, like you have been so depressed for so long that you feel the agony will never end. It is hard to finally realize that if your parent hasn't come back yet, she/he most likely never will.

Always Questions

You have questions about your parent, whether that parent has died or abandoned you, for the rest of your life. As Julie B. said, "Your parents are your parents, and, whether they are with you or not, you are always going to be curious about their lives."

Every kid has different questions about the missing parent. Noel wonders, "Would my personality have been any different if he hadn't died? I want to know all about his car accident. And what was he like and am I like him (I look just like him) and what would my mom's and his relationship be like? Would they still be together if he had not died? Would I have had as much freedom?"

Stephen, whose father left and didn't come back, said most kids would wonder things like:

What is he doing now?

Is he okay?

Is he happy?

Does he remember that I am here?

Is he alive?

Where is he?

Is he married?

Does he have kids?

Is he a bum or is he rich?

Faith said, "Not knowing is hard. A lot of the answers you will never know because they are gone forever. Some answers are difficult to find. But you need to try because it is important to your own self-respect."

Images

Noel said, "If you don't know anything about your missing parent, you might make up images in your head." One girl said, "I read about a kid who met her mother after many years. She had a picture of her mother and thought she was beautiful. When she met her mother, the vision was not what she expected." Amyee said, "My image of a father is that he is nice, he has a Ferrari, a great big mansion, and a car for every kid." Stephen said, "My image of him is that he is five feet four, brown hair, lives in a shack and has about twenty-two kids. I think he is a busy man!"

Sometimes, it is bits of memories that give you your image, as was one girl's memory of her parent: "My dad was beating up my mom. I had on a pink coat. My mom used to sleep with a knife under her pillow. Life is better because my parents don't live together, but I wish so badly that my memory was a good memory. The bad memory makes me feel hurt. I don't know anything good about him." We think this happens because, as Scott said, "Bad memories have a way of sticking." Debby said, "I sit sometimes for hours and think of what it would be like to have a father hold me, take me places, and tell me he loves me. If only I could have that feeling once more. I always see pictures with him holding me, and I get so mad at myself because I can't remember that feeling."

Our images of our missing parents are very, very important to us. It can mean the difference between liking yourself and not liking yourself. As Noel said, "If you have a bad image of your parent, you think you might grow up to be bad, too." When you hear just bad things about the parent who isn't there, you think, "Well, if my dad or my mom was no good, then no one will like me." No matter how bad parents are, kids want to know something good about them for their own benefit.

Finding Out About Your Parent

We think that the best situations are when kids feel free to talk to the parent they live with about the parent who is missing. Noel said, "My mother always answers my questions." Christie, whose father died when she was little, said, "My mom tells me good things about him. She has a film of him water-skiing. It is funny when we watch it backward."

Sometimes your parent may not be the best person to talk to because, for reasons of his/her own, that parent might not choose to have good memories. This is too bad. As Norman said, "I always wanted to talk to my mom because in a sense my mother knew him best. I never wanted to ask. I thought I would hear something bad."

We think that the parent you live with should talk to you about the missing parent. One girl said, "My mom gets so angry sometimes that she doesn't feel like talking about him, and I really get angry with my mom when she won't tell me things about him." We think every child has a right to know about a parent, although maybe not all the details if they are really hurtful.

Grandparents can sometimes be good to talk to about your missing parent. It just depends on how they feel about that parent. You might find out good things, or your grandparents might be hurt just like your parent and say something like "He was a no-good, a louse." This can really hurt you, even though sometimes you might agree with your grandparents."

Aunts and uncles can give kids good ideas of what their parents were like. Missy said, "I could talk to my aunt about my father because she and I are so much alike." Or friends of your parent can help you. Norman told us: "I talk to guys who knew my father because they understand and are easy to talk to."

When You Aren't Told the Whole Truth

The worst thing that can happen is when you are told lies about the missing parent by your other parent, friends, or relatives. Naomi said, "If this happens, you can have a distorted image of that parent." We tried to think of why you would be told lies about a parent. Sheri said, "A lot of parents might want to tell their kids bad things that aren't true so that the kids will feel glad to be with them instead of the other parents that are supposedly so evil. Parents can forget that just because they are bad for each other doesn't mean they will be bad for you."

Elizabeth had some other ideas. She said, "Parents want to protect kids. They might not want them to know the truth because they think kids might think badly of them." Or they may think they need to protect kids from seeing the other parent because they think that it would not be good for the kids. Julie B. said, "I know a kid whose parents got a divorce. The father was trying to get in touch with him, but the mother didn't want his father to see him. So she told him that his dad didn't want to see him. She lied to him for two years. When he finally found out, she couldn't explain it." As Scott said, "If you grow up and then find out the truth, it will really upset you."

Sometimes parents make agreements for the sake of the kid. One girl said, "I know a girl whose father left. The parents made a deal that the father wouldn't come around to see her because it would be upsetting for her. He may want to see her, but he stays away because he thinks he will be a bad influence." If the kid has some say in the deal, maybe it could be good, although we think that, as Julie H. said, "Not visiting at all can hurt more." Kids need contact with the other parent and need to hear about that parent. Noel said, "Just because a parent is bad doesn't mean a kid will be bad. Even parents who have done bad things can give kids some love and caring."

You sometimes hear things from the parent you live with that aren't completely lies but aren't the whole truth either. One boy said, "When they had my sister, they said that she would be the first and the last. My mother was happy when she got pregnant again, but my father wasn't. My mother got mad one time and told me that my father left because of me. She said that he would still be here if I wasn't around." It can be a pretty heavy load for a kid to carry around, and the truth is usually more complicated than that. You might even make jokes about your parent with friends or relatives. They can seem funny at the time but really hurt you and the parent who isn't there. It is important to remember that, as Norman said, "Parents may leave for their own reasons and not because of you."

A parent should remember that a lot of kids think, as one girl said, "The missing parent is still part of the family. If the parent at home doesn't want the other parent to make contact, the kid starts to think that the other parent must have done something really bad even if that parent didn't do anything. A parent might think that not seeing the other parent will make you forget about that parent, but really what happens is that it makes you want to try harder when you get older."

Some things kids need to find out on their own. Faith said, "After a few years of not seeing my dad, he showed up and wanted me to live with him. I was so happy at first. But then after a while I thought, 'If he wanted me, he would have come before this. Why did he come now and not before?' So I told him exactly what I thought. He was mad, but I couldn't let my mom down. After all, she was the one who had taken care of me for ten years. She could have left like he did, but she didn't. I think it was because she cared more, and I just wasn't going to let her down."

Ghosts

Missing parents can have a powerful impact on you even if they have been gone for a long time. Bruce said, "I think about times with him. He is still part of my life. He wanted me to go to college, and that is important to me." Bronwen said, "Sometimes I think I still talk to my mom now. If I am ever in a difficult situation, I think, 'How would Mom have handled it?'" Or people say to you, in a good way, "You are just like your mother," or "You are the spitting image of your father." These comments can make you feel very proud.

Sometimes when somebody says, "You act like your parent," it can have a double meaning. It really depends, according to Scott, on what the person who is saying it thinks about the missing parent. It can get in the way, and you really don't know what to do. It can be used to punish you. If you get into trouble, you hear things like, "Your father wouldn't have done that." Or, as Julie B. said, "Mother wouldn't do that. You are nothing like your mother. Why couldn't you be more like her?"

This can put too much pressure on a kid. Michelle said that her friend's mother died, and the father thought that her friend should be just like her, the head of the house and a perfect student. You can have a hard time making your own decisions about what to do with your life. Stephen said, "Let's say you want to grow up to play basketball. Your mother may want you to be a lawyer just like your father. You might go ahead and do this because you wouldn't want to disappoint him."

Some Suggestions That Can Help

We think there is nothing worse than dealing with the feelings that go along with having one parent gone from your life. We would like to suggest some ideas that helped us.

Try not to hate your parent. Hate, even for good reasons, can make a kid feel guilty. If you never see the parent again, you never get a chance to clear it up. Feeling hate for too long a time can make you sick inside. We think that, for kids' sakes, they need to feel some respect for both parents, even though some parents might not always deserve it. Roger, whose father left when he was nine, said, "I never saw my father again after my parents broke up. He never came to see us or did anything with us. I held a grudge against him at first. It took quite a long time to think of him as just another person I know but really don't like."

We have a lot of friends from single-parent families and almost all of them live with their mothers. Many of them resent and hate their fathers. One girl is even thinking of changing her name. Out of everything we know about kids and single-parent families, this disturbs us the most.

Hate is hard on a kid. Tina said, "I think that hate is one of the worst things because it is bad for you and is sometimes the only thing you can think about. I think it is awful to have to dislike or hate a parent. Really, you always want to be as proud of your parent as your parent is of you (sometimes)." We wonder, too, if you stop and think, whether or not a kid ever really hates a parent.

You can direct the hate at yourself sometimes. A lot of kids, even if they have been told differently and understand, always think that the reason their parent is missing is their fault. One girl said, "My mother has always told me that my father left because he had a drinking problem, and he just couldn't handle big responsibilities like a family, so I shouldn't blame myself. After thirteen years, when I talk about my father, I still blame myself. I used to think that he left because I did something to him like spitting up on his shoe. A little ways along I realize that it is *his* fault. I usually end up calling him names and saying it is his fault, but I always start out thinking that it is mine."

It might help you to think as Julie H. does. She said, "I can really feel for anyone who has just started going through all the different emotions after a divorce, but I think that the people I really feel sorry for are all of the parents who didn't want custody of their children. They don't know what they are missing."

It is possible that kids are likely to be mad at all men or all women, if they were left by the parent of that sex. Julie H. said, "You don't have to stay that way. You actually get to know men (if you were left by your father) better because you need to learn about them. When Mom comes home with a date, you learn to get along with that person and accept the fact that some guys have problems that they can't handle. But guys have good points. You learn that they do try and that they can be great to hang around with."

You may just have to accept that a parent isn't coming back and could be gone forever. This isn't easy but will help you to go on with your life. You might even have to accept the fact that your parent didn't care. You may also have to make some adjustments. Julie H. said, "You have to cry and let your feelings out. You have to scream and yell and curse at him or her. Then you have to tell yourself your parent has problems and just couldn't handle it. Sometimes you have to block your parent from your thoughts because, if you think about your parent, you will feel sad all the time."

You have to remember that you have your mother or father and other people who care about you. Amyee said, "After my parents separated, I hated my dad. I felt unwanted. Now I really hate him but don't feel unwanted because I have my mother, and she makes up for it." Stephen, whose father abandoned him when he was born, said, "It's weird because, if I bump into somebody on the street, sometimes I will wonder, 'Is that my father?' But I really have stopped thinking about it all that much. He decided to get on with his life just like I have got to get on with mine. Life is too short to wonder about somebody who doesn't care about me."

You are going to have many fantasies about you and your missing parent, but you have to realize they are most likely not going to come true. We guess all you can do is just keep dreaming. Debby said, "When I hear my friends talk about all the fun they have with their fathers, I really enjoy it. I have never experienced this feeling. All I can do is dream about the fun I could have with my father."

You may never get completely over a missing parent, but you can be happy. You still have one parent and can work to make a life with that parent. Try to comfort your parent and show that parent your love.

MAKING SPECIAL FRIENDS

A lot of times when people talk about a friend who is like a father or who is like a mother to a kid, they say, "He is a good substitute," or "She is a good substitute." This word doesn't make sense to us. It is true that someone can be a very good friend, even a special friend, but we don't think that anyone can be a "substitute." As Stephen and Norman agreed, "Nobody could ever really take your parent's place."

It is true though that, after a few years, kids can find people in their lives who become special and helpful to them in a way that a parent can be. Julie H. said, "Well, I do have other parent figures, mostly adult friends. I call them Mom or Dad if I feel comfortable enough." Kids look for special adults because their single parents often have their hands full and because they just think they have a gap in their lives they need to fill. They look for people who can care about them and maybe take on some of the responsibility in their lives. Kids whose parents have divorced or kids who have had a parent die look for adult friends.

It could be one of your parent's friends, a boyfriend, a girl-friend, or maybe a stepparent. A lot of times it is a relative who wants to get closer to you. Darcey said, "After my father died, I got really close to my uncle. I would stay at his house sometimes and do things with him. He is excellent for me, and I love him." It can be easier and more comfortable if you have an aunt or uncle around because they know you already, and you won't be as shy. A lot of times, aunts and uncles have a better understanding of what is going on in your life. The important thing is that you feel good about the person and feel that you are safe in the relationship, whether the person is a relative or not.

A lot of us thought that if the friend was the same sex as you, it would be easier. Norman pointed out that, "The person would have a better idea of what you are going through." It seems most important, though, that the person be interested in what you are interested in and, if that is the case, the sex of the person doesn't really matter. It is helpful, too, if the person is somewhat older than you. We guessed that really anybody older than twenty years could be good. As Norman said, "Kids need older friends to talk to and let feelings out with. There are some things that you just can't talk to younger people about."

If brothers or sisters are older than you and take care of you a lot, they can become like parents to you as well. Faith said, "When I was ten, I always used to consider my brother as the closest thing to a father. He used to take care of me and help my mother with the money. She would worry a lot about not having enough money for the bills. When he left home, I felt like it was my real father leaving, and I felt hurt and deserted."

Sometimes brothers and sisters can also become special friends to you. You have gone through life together in a single-parent family and often get closer. You learn to need each other more by listening and understanding, or at least trying to understand, each other's feelings. Amyee said, "Older kids can answer younger kids' questions about the divorce or the death." You can help each other out with problems like being bored or lonesome or sad about the missing parent.

It is easy to be afraid to have special feelings for another adult. Kids can feel guilty about those feelings. One girl said, "When I first realized that I didn't have a father, my uncle all of a sudden came into the picture. I was really happy, but then I thought, 'This has to stop because I have a real father, and he still loves me.'" Another reason is that a kid just might be stubborn. You might carry the idea that no one can take your parent's place too far.

Special friends are important to a kid. They can be there to listen, help you sort out your feelings, give you suggestions, and offer solutions to problems. You can go places like ball games, movies, or stores. As Stephen said, "Even if they don't take you places, they are good to talk to."

THE DREAM NEVER GOES AWAY

"My little sister is the youngest. She was most hurt by the divorce although she didn't show it at the time. Maybe she couldn't accept it. I don't know. It is hitting her now, two years later. When my dad would date other people she would say, 'Oh, they are going to get married, and we are going to be a family again.' When it didn't happen and she finally realized it, she had a very hard time." —A fourteen-year-old girl.

Even after a few years, the dream that your parents are going to get back together or that a dead parent will be alive again doesn't completely go away. Laura said, "You think about it in the day, and you dream about it at night." Or you might see things that remind you of the dream. Julie H. said, "My mother put all her wedding pictures in a drawer at our house. There are things in the drawer that we use every day. Sometimes when I see them, I want to cry. I want my parents to be together again. I think to myself, 'Why doesn't she throw the pictures away?' "

Some times of the year are harder on us than others. Darcey said, "If you are going someplace special or if it is a birthday or holiday, you get into these moods where you think, 'Gee, it would be fun if my parents were back together.' "

Julie B. said, "It gets you mad when you want to do things with both parents. I can't do that. When I hear about other kids with two parents saying, 'Guess what? We just came back from the beach with our parents,' it makes me want to get my father and mother back together again." Dora said, "Two of my best friends at school live with both of their parents. I am not really jealous of them. Sometimes though, I think, 'Oh no, I don't want to talk about it.' "

One girl described her own thinking: "You still think of yourself as a family even if you are not living together. You may not be seeing each other at all. In your thoughts your parents still love you and care about each other no matter where everybody is. You hang on to a dead parent or to a parent who has abandoned you."

Even in families where divorced parents end up getting along pretty well, you still wish for more. Julie B. said, "We still are a family in a way but not really. At Thanksgiving we all get together. Then it feels most like a family, but a different kind of family. My mother and father get along very well when they are together, but in real families, parents kiss and hug each other, and my parents don't."

WE THINK SINGLE PARENTS HAVE COURAGE

Regardless of what parents decide or how they have changed, most of us see our parents, after a few years of single-parent living, as having "courage." Many of us have watched our parents set goals and be sure and positive about their lives and feelings. We are impressed with the way that single parents get back on their feet after a divorce or a death and don't let it get them down. Amyee said, "I feel that my mom has guts. She managed to raise good kids without being too hard. I am amazed that she can put up with us by herself without having a nervous breakdown. Not only that, she has supported us without any financial help from my father."

We have learned that that single parents supporting their kids is one way that they show their love. And, after a few years in single-parent families, we have realized that getting closer to our parents is an opportunity we could have missed.

5

ABC's of
Single-Parent Families

AFFECTION AND LOVE

It is so hard to describe a feeling with words. Love is a happy feeling you get when you are with someone you really care about. It is a deep affection and understanding of another person. It means that when someone you love needs you, you will be there for that person. Love is everything good mixed up together. Don't ask us how a cat would describe love. It would probably just lick your face.

We need love for everything: to hope, to feel secure, to care about living, and even to hate. Without love in a family, everyone ends up at each other's throat. People who are completely without love go crazy or become physically sick.

Our parents do a lot of things to let us know that we are loved. They hug us and spend time with us. They care about our schoolwork. They treat us like people and not just kids. They give us kisses before we go to bed at night and make us favorite meals for dinner. They talk to us. Noel said, "My mom sits down with me and tells me about personal things."

When we feel loved, we act differently. Naomi said, "I am nice to my friends and feel like being with people. I get sudden urges to call up a friend and invite him/her over." We smile a lot and are less likely to hurt someone else's feelings. Faith said, "I act funny and tell stupid jokes." Noel said, "I feel excited and happy." Margae said, "My mom and I walk on each other's feet, and my dad and I joke around."

We make better family members when we feel loved. We are more likely to do the things that our parents ask us to do. We are nicer to brothers and sisters also. Naomi said, "When I feel loved, I don't fight with my sister. I play games with her and don't care if she spells a word wrong and still wants points for it." Our dogs and cats do better, too. They are more likely to get treated with affection and gentleness, get played with, and even get brushed.

Feeling like you need love is painful. When this happens, we feel sad, needy, put down, and, as Norman said, "left out and out of place." We mope around and hint about things we want. Often, we will go out of our way to irritate somebody. Margae said, "When I feel unloved, I usually feel depressed, like no one cares. I start thinking the world is full of a bunch of icky people."

We all try to get love one way or another. One girl said, "Sometimes when I am really down, I call my boyfriend, and we talk for a while. Then I just say, 'Do you really love me?' He usually says, 'Yes.' Then I am really happy, and it gives me a good feeling." We think the best way to feel loved is just to ask for it. Missy said, "Just get up and get a hug from your parent." For some reason hugging is something *all* of us think does the job.

Asking for love is scary. But no matter how hard it is, it is your job to make sure that you get the love you need, even if it means coming right out and saying, "I'm really down in the dumps" or something like that. If your mom or dad isn't available, friends and relatives will do. Grandparents especially are very good at giving love. *(See* GRANDPARENTS.)

Remember, too, there are times when you will get shown love in ways that don't always feel good. Parents may stop you from doing things that they think are dangerous. Sheri said, "One time my mother wouldn't let me go skiing because she was afraid I would get hurt." And Julie H. said, "I remember once my mom made me stay home from a party because she wasn't sure about how safe I would be." Also, there are times that parents might hurt your feelings by telling you the truth about one of your friends. Maybe a friend has lied or stolen. We know that parents are just trying to protect us, but it always feels bad when it happens.

It is important for kids to bring love into their families. Kids need to let parents and brothers and sisters know that they are loved. Spending time with them or doing special things for them is good. One girl said, "Sometimes I buy my mother a red rose, and we sit and talk about good times that we have had." Tina said, "Once I cooked a big meal for all of us, and it really made a difference." And Amyee said, "Sometimes just being funny and keeping everybody laughing is a way to let people know you love them."

We think that everybody needs love. Feeling loved helps you to get through life. Elizabeth said, "Every day you need people to tell you they love you. You need to know you are cared about so that you can believe in yourself."

ALCOHOL

Alcoholism is the cause of many single-parent families through divorce and death. And, as Elizabeth said, "Even when the alcoholic parent is home, it is like that parent isn't there. The parent is almost always 'buzzed' and doesn't act at all like a parent. One parent is raising the kid and the other is destroying him/herself."

Alcoholism is a disease that can *never* be cured but only temporarily quenched.

Once a person has been an alcoholic, they will always be tempted to revert back to drinking. Sometimes people make up excuses why they should drink. They say things like "Nobody loves me" or "You made me do it." But that is not the real reason they drink. As Noel said, "They drink because they drink."

Adults become alcoholic, and kids become alcoholic. Most people drink as a way to escape from the pressures of life. Kids often drink too much because of peer pressure to drink. As Stephen said, "Sometimes kids get so confused that the pressure takes them over."

Many kids who have alcohol problems have parents who have alcohol problems. Evita Cobo, a therapist with the Substance

Abuse Program at United Counseling Service, thought this was true in 75 percent of the cases where kids have serious alcohol problems. We think, too, that kids who live in a single-parent family, where the pressure can be greater, might be more likely to drink, especially when they are having to deal with the loss of a parent who has moved away or died.

You can know (but sometimes deny) when parents are alcoholic. Their whole personality is quite different and their physical appearance is affected. Some parents become drunk and come home "staggering drunk" and get into big fights with the family. Others become very withdrawn. You don't have to be drunk all the time to be alcoholic. It's a question of what effect drinking too much has on you when you do it.

We made up two typical scenes that are disturbing to kids with alcoholic parents. We thought they would give you an idea of the way that kids see life with an alcoholic.

Scene 1

"It is Friday night. All the kids in the family are going to a party. The daughter brings a friend to the house. When they get there, the mother is drunk and starts to fight with her, almost violently. Her friend leaves, and her little brother starts screaming. The mother starts yelling about never getting respect and starts hitting everyone."

Scene 2

"A girl comes home one day and finds her father drunk and depressed (her mother just died). She hides his bottle of whiskey. He is drinking with a friend and gets mad when he can't find the bottle. He and the friend start fighting. The girl feels sorry for her father and thinks that he is weak for having to drink so much. She starts to worry that he will try to kill himself and quickly calls her grandmother."

An alcoholic in the family has lasting and drastic effects on you. If your parent is alcoholic, you might learn to drink just like the parent. You might see your parent use alcohol as an escape and decide to be just like that parent. You might even start drinking with the parent.

If you live in a single-parent family with an alcoholic parent, it makes it even worse. Essentially, you are on your own, and it makes you grow up too fast. You usually feel guilty, like the drinking is all your fault. Kids who live with alcoholics become ashamed of themselves and the parent. Most of the time, they feel angry that the parent is ruining his/her life and their life, too.

Your schoolwork can go downhill, and your social life can end. You just stop inviting friends to stay over, and you tell them lies to keep from being embarrassed. A lot of kids put up a front of nothing being wrong. You "don't want friends to see your parent when they are in one of their drunken stages." It is awful having to apologize. It feels better just not taking the chance of getting in that spot.

You find yourself covering up for parents by making excuses and taking on the responsibilities. You are likely to become "the mother" or "the father" to younger children in the family. You may take on cooking responsibilities or housework. You are always wondering, "What will my parent do next?" or "How can I help my parent?" You think about what to tell people who call for your parent. Usually, kids think they are helping out. They feel sorry for the parent. In fact, they are only enabling the parent to keep drinking.

Ms. Cobo said, "A lot of kids with alcoholic parents get into trouble as a way of getting the attention that they don't feel they are getting. Or they become 'clowns' in the family. They keep everything light and not serious as a way to keep the pain away." Other kids leave the house every chance that they get and just withdraw from the family.

It is common for kids who live with alcoholic parents to *never* drink because of the damage that they see happen around them.

One girl told us: "I don't think I will ever drink. I have had to watch my parent hurt herself, and I don't want my kids to go through what I have." But if one of your parents is an alcoholic, you are more likely to marry an alcoholic. This is because you have carried the burden for so long that you think you are supposed to continue it.

There are places to go for help if one of your parents is an alcoholic. Julie H. said, "Kids shouldn't be embarrassed to ask for help. You just have to face the fact that it is happening. In some towns, the Alateen program can help you (look it up in your phone book). Or, if you can't find Alateen, call Al-Anon. You can get group help for living with an alcoholic parent from either organization, and you can go there whether your parent has stopped drinking or not."

It is important to talk to other people about the problem and not keep it bottled up inside of you. You could try to talk to close friends, the other parent, or other adult friends. One girl told us: "I always talk to my boyfriend, my aunts, or my grandmother." Kids need to remember that sometimes relatives are not always the best people to talk to about the problem. They might be as frightened as the alcoholic and not believe what you tell them. Often, your other parent will deny it as much as the alcoholic parent. You shouldn't stop there if this happens.

Kids could always call mental health centers. Ms. Cobo said, "If kids call us, first I listen to them. It is really important for them to know that they can tell someone about the problem. I make sure I tell them it is not their fault. I try to get them to step back and not take on too much responsibility for getting the parent to stop drinking."

These are some thoughts about how to handle yourself if your parent is drinking too much:

Don't hide the bottle

Leave the parent alone

Hint that the parent needs outside help

Ask relatives for advice

Don't argue with a drunken parent

Think about living somewhere else until the parent stops
drinking

If your parent is alcoholic, it is important that the parent get
help as well. This is a hard job if you are a kid. If you try to
confront a parent about the drinking, you will get denial from that
parent. This is when a parent refuses to believe that he/she has a
problem. Oftentimes, if you approach a parent, you will get told to
"lay off" or "stop bugging me." Even worse, trying to help can be
dangerous. You can get abused easily when a parent is drunk.

Trying to do it on your own is, as one girl told us, "just wasting
your time." It feels frustrating to kids when they keep offering to
help and the parent refuses. You have to realize that you can't cure
your parent by yourself. The truth is that too often a person has to
get to a point where it hurts so badly that he/she wants help. Tom
said, "A lot of times something really bad happens before they
realize that they need help, like getting into a car accident and
killing someone."

People can get help before a tragedy happens, but it takes
adult friends to get that parent professional help from counselors or
at detoxification centers or from Alcoholics Anonymous. Professionals know ways of getting the alcoholic into treatment before
something awful happens. Ms. Cobo told us, "Counselors can do
something called an intervention. This is when family members
and others who are concerned about the alcoholic get together as a
group to confront the alcoholic with the problem. It is a group
effort."

Often an alcoholic of any age will need to go to a residential
treatment center. Ms. Cobo told us about it. "It is like a hospital.
The alcoholic gets educated about alcohol. They go through a lot of
group therapy with other people who are trying to stop drinking.
The family gets involved, too, because alcoholism is really a family

problem. Family members need to change as well, and the treatment center helps everybody with how they are going to change."

Don't feel bad if you hate the alcoholic parent while that parent is drinking. When the drinking stops, you will probably love that parent again.

ANGER: KIDS

How do you know when you are angry? You know you are angry when:

You yell and scream
Feel like vomiting
Want to punch a wall
Cry your heart out
Or tense up like you want to hit somebody

When you are angry, your body feels nervous and trembly, you quiver all over and your stomach gets tied in knots. Maybe you know that you are angry when you don't feel like talking to anyone and sulk a lot, or you feel guilty about something. Anger can make you have scary thoughts. One girl said, "Sometimes I wish that my mother was dead. (I don't really mean it, though.)" Thoughts like these are normal as long as you don't *do* what you are thinking.

Every kid gets angry differently. When some kids get mad, they get angry with anyone and everyone. Others don't ever get mad at anyone but themselves. Certain kids get angry only with specific people, like a mother or a stepparent.

Some kids do really stupid things when they are angry, sometimes dangerous things. Scott said, "The stupidest thing I ever did was to get mad, throw a rock, and split open a friend's head." Michelle said, "I broke a bottle over my cousin's friend's feet." You can do things you wish you hadn't done. Tom told us: "One time I was so angry that I ripped up some important papers of mine."

Occasionally, you do just ridiculous things. Jenny said, "Once I yelled at a babysitter and told her that I wouldn't take a shower unless the television was plugged in."

There are kids who hold all their anger inside. This can be good if in your anger you would say or do something to hurt someone. One girl said, "When my sister gets all the attention, I feel like beating her up!" But holding in anger can hurt you. Usually, what happens is that the tension builds up. Then you start exaggerating little things people around you do and take it out on them. Michelle said, "One of my friends holds her anger in so long that after a while every little thing gets to her so she cries." Finally, you can't hold it in anymore, and you let it out. Scott said, "I do it all the time. Believe me, it is not good for you. You literally blow up sometimes."

If you think this might happen, the best thing is, as Jenny said, "to just go somewhere alone and cry or talk to yourself. If that doesn't work, it might be good to go talk to someone else." Friends can help you with anger. Stephen said, "I have a friend who I have a deal with. I get to scream at him and hit him to let off steam. Then, we are still friends, and I feel better. It is fun."

Every family has a "pecking order." For example, Jenny lives in a two-parent house: "First, my brother gets mad, he takes it out on me, I take it out on Kris, Kris gets mad at Sharon, Sharon yells at my father, my mother gets it next, my mother either stops it right there or the dog gets it." Scott lives in a stepfamily. "It goes Dad, Mom, me, Eric, Dad, Mom." Tom lives in a single-parent family, and his works a little differently. "I yell at my brother, and then he picks on my sister. After that, everybody gets grumpy, and my mother yells at us all."

Kids in single-parent families do have things to get mad about that other kids don't, like a parent being gone, a working parent, maybe a lack of money or food, and more competition with brothers and sisters. The hardest thing is to give up anger that you have had for a long time. This is usually anger at missing parents. We think that the more you know about the reasons your parent is gone, the better you will feel. As Julie H. said, "Ask all the questions that are in your mind. The sooner you find out that it isn't your fault, the sooner it will probably start to go away."

The anger can make you feel like drinking sometimes or taking drugs. Some kids might even overdose because they are angry. They can't take it anymore so they turn to drugs. We say, "Why take drugs? Find a friend and talk it over. Drugs just screw up your brain anyway. Talk to anybody, just don't do it."

Michelle said, "It is possible to control your anger; you just have to learn mind and emotion control." Playing sports is helpful for getting rid of anger. And so is writing in your diary. It can give you a private person to talk to. Treating yourself well by doing your favorite thing works, too.

ANGER: PARENTS

Every parent gets angry at one time or another.

Single parents get angry for a number of reasons. A lot of single parents get frustrated because they have to do everything themselves. Sheri thought, "The extra responsibilities they have put a lot of pressure on them." Some are angry because they don't want to accept the responsibility of their situation. Most single parents get angry only some of the time, like anybody else. The ones who are angry *all* the time are the ones who, as Darcey suggested, "just aren't satisfied with the way of life."

It isn't hard to tell when parents are angry. Amyee said, "Their face gets all red, and they start complaining and yelling at you." Darcey said another way to tell is "when a parent just won't talk to you." Or a parent might do things like "stomp around," "slam things down," or "scream."

A lot of times parents try to pretend they are not angry when they really are. You can almost always tell. When parents are trying to pretend, their voices are a little higher. They say that they aren't angry but won't talk to you. Or, as Amyee said, "They are acting nice but they are saying the wrong things and their faces are still red!"

Kids feel worst when parents take anger out on them. One girl said, "Some days my mom comes home and just starts yelling about *nothing*. That makes me feel like I am worthless." When parents are angry, they can say really, really bad things, and they hurt. Debby said, "One day I was in a hurry and dropped a dish. My mother got so mad at me that I started to cry."

Kids are affected by a parent's anger. Darcey said, "A kid picks up all the things that a parent does. If a parent is always angry, oftentimes a kid will probably be mad, too." Amyee thought, "When parents are angry, kids are more likely to get mad at their friends. Some start fighting more." Almost all kids feel hurt, upset, sad, alone, or scared when a parent is angry.

A lot of times kids don't understand when a parent gets angry. You think, "They have no reason to act like that." And, as Julie B. said, "You probably think that the parent is angry because of you." Then you think, "Why are they mad? Is it me? Will I ever see my parent happy again?"

Anger isn't always bad. Debby said, "One time, I broke my mother's toe. She got so mad at me that she swore. I ran off to my room. My mom came running after me, and that day was the first day we had hugged in five years."

You and your parent can get to know each other better because of anger. Sheri said, "One time I got a C-plus on a test. My mom was really angry. She told me that I didn't try and could have gotten an A-plus if I had wanted to. I felt like I had let everyone down, and I was upset. The day after she was still mad, and I started to cry. She told me that she was sorry and that I was doing my best even though she would like me to work harder. Then, I don't know why, we just started laughing. Now she only gets a little mad when I get a bad grade."

The most important thing is what parents do with their anger. When some parents get angry, they can drink too much, use drugs, or hit kids. Other parents get angry when they actually are sad. One girl said, "My mom and I fight a lot. One time her dog was lost, and she thought it was my fault. I didn't like the dog. We looked for him for two days. My mother started to cry and said that the dog was the only one who really cared about her. I felt really bad."

If parents can talk over their anger with the people they are angry with and figure out ways to solve the problem, it is better. If that doesn't work, Sheri suggested, "Parents should find a way to take a vacation to take some of the pressure off."

It is hard to know the best thing to do when a parent is angry. Julie B. said, "One night my mother came home and started yelling at me so I started yelling back. That made her really angry." Sometimes you get angry back and can't stop yourself. As Darcey said, "you think, 'I am going to regret this. Why am I doing it?' " Often it is best just to let the parent have some time alone to get over the anger.

ATTENTION

We all had different opinions on what age kids need the most attention and why:

Tom said, "They need the most attention when they are little because they can't take care of themselves."

Scott said, "Kids three or four years old need the most attention because they are always into mischief."

Sheri said, "Kids need the most during their teenage years because things are changing all around them—schools, people, and friends. They need someone to talk to about problems and changes."

Darcey thought the same thing and added, "If kids don't get attention at that age, they might start some bad habits."

And then we thought about what our parents are like when they don't get enough attention. Some get mean and angry or irritable and cranky. Others get grumpy and yell a lot. One boy said, "Everyone yells and fights, and I end up getting in trouble." Julie B. said, "My mother gets very discouraged."

In the end, we agreed with Jenny, who said, "People just don't ever grow out of the need for attention. Without any attention, people will fall apart." Michelle added, "It is a big part of growing up."

Good attention makes people feel, as Tom said, "great." Sheri said, "It makes you feel secure and wanted, loved and comforted, just plain good." Michelle said, "You feel like you are noticed." Scott told us, "It makes you feel like you are a somebody, somebody who people like." And Darcey said, "You feel as if you don't have a worry in the world."

There are a lot of ways to try to get attention. One way kids use is being bad. They do things like pick on brothers and sisters, swear, or drop things. In their minds, they say, "I want attention," so they go into the television room and start a fight with someone. A lot of kids throw temper tantrums as a way to get attention. To stop the tantrum, the parent has to give a kid some time. If the parent yells, the tantrum only gets worse. Amyee said, "For some kids, this is the only kind of attention that they know."

Kids will use tricky ways to get attention. Some show off. Scott told us, "I remember my fourth birthday party. I tied a towel around myself and jumped off the steps. I landed on a coffee table and ended up in the hospital." Some try becoming a nuisance. One boy told us about a method he uses when he is feeling neglected: "Hanging on your parent is great. Let's say your parent is working in the kitchen. You go into the kitchen and hang all over your parent. The parent usually doesn't like it, but it does the job." Other kids will be very quiet or pretend to be sick.

Most kids try to get attention by being very good. As Jenny said, "It feels good if you get attention from doing something good, and if you get attention from doing something bad, you aren't satisfied." You may get good grades in school or work hard at home to get the attention you want. You may do things that aren't expected of you, like vacuuming the floor or changing the beds. Amyee gave an example: "The other night I was doing the dishes. My brother got yelled at for not taking out the garbage, and my sister yelled at my mother because she didn't want to do the laundry. I just kept doing the dishes. My mom thanked me for not yelling."

Upsetting to us is that some kids become desperate for attention. They feel lonely, left out, and not liked by other people. They do things like getting pregnant, breaking the law, or trying to commit suicide (not really wanting to die). They get into trouble as a way to get even with a parent and to hurt them. They don't get the kind of attention they hoped for, but, at the time, they think it is better than none.

Whether you get more or less attention living in a single-parent family depends on the family situation and the parent. In some single-parent families, kids find it easier to get more good attention because they don't have to compete with another parent for time. And if your parent still feels guilty, you often get more attention because your parent is always trying to make up for the guilt. But when a single parent has to work all the time, there is usually less attention to go around.

Kids in every family compete for attention. In fact, kids compete for attention in any way that they have to. If being bad gets attention, kids will compete by being bad. Amyee said, "My brother gets attention when he is bad. I think, 'If he can do it, I can do it.' " These are some situations we think would most likely cause a lot of competition for attention:

A stepchild and a natural child
A brother and sister
The oldest and the youngest
One parent with two or more kids
When a parent has a boyfriend or a girlfriend

Some kids really like to compete, but many kids find that "it is hard and frustrating." They can feel guilty competing for attention because, even when they get it, they think that they got it the wrong way.

We believe it is important for kids to get the same amount of attention from a parent. Kids don't like it when parents "play favorites." Sheri told us about a time that she didn't get enough attention: "My aunt, uncle, two cousins, and I went to a fair. I felt that they didn't care what rides or games I did but really cared about my cousins." This can make a kid feel "rotten." We think that every kid wants, as Sheri said, "To be loved, to have time to talk and open up to a parent, and to do special things alone with that parent." This is true even if the parent has a boyfriend or a girlfriend. Attention, to a kid, is when a parent talks to you even though there are other people around, like your friends or your parent's date. It means keeping the conversation fair.

We think the best way for kids to get attention is to ask for it. This can be hard sometimes. Dora said, "Sometimes I say, 'Hey, I don't get that much close time with you.' We get into fights about it, and we may end up screaming at each other. It helps. It can be the only way we communicate about these things. A lot of times my mom doesn't do anything different. She listens and still doesn't spend time with me. But at least she knows."

Asking for attention might make you feel, as Norman said, "like a little kid," but it is better than getting into trouble or hurting yourself. You might even be able to make deals with your parent for attention if time is short. Julie B. said, "One time I cleaned the whole house, and my mom and I went out to eat together in return." Elizabeth said, "When two or more kids have something going on at the same time, you have a problem. So far, our family hasn't solved this problem yet. A good way though would be for the kids to compromise so that the parent could do one thing at a time with one kid and the next time with another." Or, if your parent isn't available, there are always friends and relatives or brothers and sisters. The most important thing to know is just that you need good attention from someone.

It is important for kids to remember also that parents need attention as much as you do. Most parents want kids to talk to them about what is going on in their lives. As Tom said, "Parents don't like to be ignored." You can listen to them, love them, and respect them. You can even help them solve some problems. Parents also like to have fun with you. It is important for them to know that if anything goes wrong, you would be there for them, just as they would be there for you. Jenny said, "That can make your parent and you feel good."

CHILD ABUSE

Child abuse can happen in any family, not just in single-parent families. It is a growing problem, and it is important that kids get help before abuse gets too bad.

There are different kinds of abuse. You can be sexually abused or physically beaten or neglected. One girl talked to us about what happened to her: "I had to kneel in a corner for three or four hours at a time. My mom would smack me on the face. I would get bruised on one side, and she would keep me home from school."

Maybe you are not being well cared for or not getting medical attention. Faith told us: "I have a friend who nobody liked when they first met her. Kids picked on her in the schoolyard because her clothes weren't as high-class as everybody else's. She had problems at home. At school, she would look empty."

There is also emotional abuse. This is when you are called names or have games played with your mind by parents. Maybe your parents don't talk to you, love you, and nurture you. This can make you feel as bad as when you are physically abused. One girl asked herself, "Who am I? I think I am dead. I think I wasn't even brought up. I am a human being, I think. I don't know who I am or what I am doing. When I wake up, am I alive or am I dead? Who cares? Some people do. Some people don't."

We interviewed Charles Gingo, the director of the Vermont Department of Social and Rehabilitative Services in our county. His agency's job is to provide services for families where child abuse is a problem. He is an expert on child abuse. Our interview with him was very helpful, and much of what we will say here we learned from him.

We were most interested in abuse and single-parent families. Surprisingly enough, we found out that the majority of situations where kids are abused are two-parent families and not single-parent families. What is important is that kids from single-parent families stand a greater chance of being abused even though there are more kids from two-parent families who are abused.

We wondered why any parents would abuse a kid. There are lots of different reasons. Parents can abuse because of not knowing how to treat or take care of kids. Some parents are very good with small kids but do not know how to handle adolescents. Or it can be the other way around. Most parents who abuse their children were abused as children themselves. The majority of these parents don't like what they are doing but don't know where to turn.

A lot of times abuse happens because of pressure. In one-parent families, the pressure can build up faster because one parent is trying to do the job of two. It is just a lot easier to run out of steam, get frustrated, and take it out on the kids. In two-parent families, a parent might have lost a job, or a wealthy parent might be having business problems. Maybe there are just too many kids to take care of. When these things happen, doors start closing and the tension builds up. *(see* ANGER: PARENTS.)

A parent can get depressed and frightened *(see* DEPRESSION: PARENTS) when the options are running out. A parent might just "shut down" and stop setting limits at home. Kids then get in control of the situation and don't really want to be.

One of the common things involved in parents abusing their kids is alcohol. Most families that come to the attention of the authorities because of child abuse have someone in the family with an alcohol problem (*see* Alcohol).

Regardless of the kind of family a kid comes from or what the cause is, most kids are afraid to talk about abuse. It is harder to talk about some kinds of abuse more than others, and the hardest one to talk about is sexual abuse.

As Mr. Gingo told us, "It is part of the whole circle. A person (parent, aunt, uncle, stranger) is abusing a child and swears the child to secrecy. The person threatens the child and says things like 'I will kill you' or 'I will break your arm' or 'I won't love you anymore.' " One girl told us that her mother said to her, "If you report me, you had better look behind you because you will be six feet under." Kids put adults on a pedestal and don't see themselves as equals. A kid thinks, "No one will believe me, and even if they do, it will be in the papers. I will get hurt, or my parent will hate me."

Mr. Gingo told us that it doesn't matter what a kid does to bring on abuse: the child is always the victim. There is no good reason why a parent should hurt a kid's body because the parent is angry. It is even possible for a kid to be a brat, and that is still not a good reason to abuse. Adults are supposed to know better. He said that many abused children become "unmanageable," get into trouble, and go to court. More than likely, the kids become unmanageable because of what the parents have done.

If you are being abused, you will have feelings like "I wish I was never born" or "It's all my fault." You might think you are a rotten person because of the things that have been said to you. You should talk to someone (teacher, friend, guidance counselor) you trust. There is a law in our state that says that certain people, like nurses, doctors, and schoolteachers, *have* to report child abuse if they suspect that it is happening.

We think you should do something about it because:

You need to protect yourself

Families can get better with help

You won't be as likely to do it to your kids

When you do report that you are being abused, things will get scary. You might even want to call the whole thing off because you are so scared. A lot of people will get involved—police, judges, lawyers, social workers. You should cooperate with them because they just want to help. If the people who are helping think the situation is serious, you may even go into a foster family.

It is always hard to go into a foster family. Not every foster family may feel right for you. Faith told us, "When my mom had to go into the hospital, I had to live with foster parents. These people were mean. I really felt left out. I wanted my mother. I used to think to myself, 'I want my mommy.' It may seem childish, but it isn't. It must feel like that for any kid who goes to live with foster parents."

A foster family can be good for some kids, though. Faith told us more about her friend: "When she first started living with her foster family, she changed. People started liking her for what she was. When she was living with her mother, she used to come into school late and used to be mean to people."

Often kids end up stronger when they get help. They become the motivators in the family for a change because they don't want to live this way any longer. Some kids are scarred for life because of the abuse they have received. Others breeze right through after they have gotten help. That is the hope.

COUNSELING

"Counseling for kids has a bad reputation, much of which isn't true. This is too bad because a lot of people could be helped, but this stereotype of counseling gets in the way."—Margae, age fourteen

A lot of kids (and grown-ups) think that counseling is only for "sick" or crazy people. They think that something is wrong with them if they ask for help. Kids especially believe that, if they go to counseling, their friends will think that they are crazy. Many people think counseling is just a waste of time and money and will only worsen things. Some people don't think about it at all but have just decided that, as Norman said, "it stinks." They are often the people who won't go because they have an idea that counselors are just people who want to "butt in" on their business. Tina said, "Actually, these are the people who need it the most."

People are often afraid of counselors because they don't understand what a counselor does. A counselor is a person who has devoted his or her career to helping people. There are different kinds of counselors: psychiatrists, psychologists, and social workers. They are considered professional counselors.

Counseling is listening and giving advice. Sometimes the advice comes from the counselor, and sometimes it comes from you after you have talked about the problem. A lot of times going to counseling means just getting out feelings, and that is what helps you.

There are different kinds of counseling situations. There is family counseling where everyone goes together to work out a problem. The good thing about family counseling, as Noel told us, is that "One person wouldn't be trying to change everything. The whole family could pitch in, and you can hear every side." Often, the problem relates to the whole family and not just to one person in the family.

Mom: I try to talk to her. She says that I treat her like a baby. Don't you?

Kid: Yeah.

Mom: She goes out with her boyfriend, drinks, and gets into trouble with the car. Isn't that right?

Kid: No!

Mom: Do you *know* the dangers of drinking and driving?

Kid: Yeah.

Mom: (To counselor) I was recently divorced. She doesn't visit her father.

Counselor: (To kid) Is that okay with you?

Kid: I don't want to see him or talk to him. My father hates me. It's like I don't exist. He never calls. I ask to see him, and he says, "Sure, sure," then nothing ever happens. I gave up on him years ago. He won't listen. Forget it, it's going nowhere.

Counselor: Have you talked to him about your feelings?

Kid: I tried it once. It didn't work. I explained what I felt like. I gave him four thousand chances when he lived at home. He sort of ignored me then, too.

When the family is in counseling, many things can come out of the discussion that had never been mentioned before.

Sometimes a kid's need for counseling means that divorced parents have to come to counseling together. This might happen in a really serious situation like when a kid has attempted suicide. Or, if a kid is having trouble being the go-between for parents, they might all get together to stop this way of communicating.

Group counseling is when you talk to peers about things that bother you. This is sometimes easiest for kids because they feel more secure talking to people their own age who have similar pressures on them. Kids can often accept advice more easily from other kids who are the same age or a little older than themselves.

Individual counseling is with just you and the counselor. Teenagers like to go alone. Margae said, "For a teenager, it can be better for one person to go at a time. Then, if you still need it, put everybody together and counsel them." Everybody has different thoughts about which one is the best for any particular situation. Regardless of which type of counseling you or your family uses, in the end you should feel like you have more choices.

Kids can feel intimidated by counselors. A lot of kids think that counselors will tell their parents what they said and get them in trouble (this is against the law unless you are in danger). Kids are also afraid that they will, as Derek said, "get the twenty-question treatment." Or instead of advice, you will get a lecture. It can be hard for kids to trust adults because they can't believe that adults understand their world. We made up a scene that shows the way a counselor can turn off a kid.

Kid: My mother ignores me.

Counselor: You could wash dishes with your mother so you could have time to talk to her.

Kid: She doesn't like me. Besides, it isn't my job to do the dishes. My brother washes the dishes. My mother never has any free time. She has three jobs and works twenty-four hours a day.

Counseling doesn't always work every time for everyone. Also, you have to remember that counseling can take time. You might have to get to know your counselor before you feel like talking about very personal things. A good counselor will give you time to get comfortable before he/she expects you to open up.

Kids feel most comfortable with counselors who act like friends. They seem like they want to talk to you, and you can tell when that is so. You feel like the counselor is talking *with* you and not *at* you. This makes you relax. If you are having trouble finding a counselor who fits for you, it is important to keep trying to talk to someone. Just don't bottle up the feelings.

We tried to decide on an ideal arrangement for kids to get counseling. A lot of the ways that counseling is offered frightens kids away. For example, a hospital setting makes kids uncomfortable. You worry that it is not private enough for you. One of the hardest things for kids is if other kids see them go to counseling. Restaurants or even a home would be better. Actually, we think the best would be under a shady tree in the park.

There are some things that you need to decide before you go to counseling. Kids should think about whether or not they want to see a man or a woman in counseling. It just depends on the kid. There are times when a girl feels more comfortable with a woman and a boy with a man. It can be just the opposite, though. The important things are whether or not you are comfortable talking to the person and you feel understood. If the problem you are having is with a man, it might be a good idea to see a man, or, if the problem is with a woman, you might want to see a woman.

It is often harder for boys to go to counseling than girls. Norman told us about his experience: "When my mother suggested counseling, I flipped out. Every time she wanted us to go, I threatened to run away." Boys are often expected to play the role of a manly independent person. This means that they are supposed to be able to handle things no matter how difficult they may really be. Society says that boys aren't supposed to show their feelings. What happens is that boys aren't expected to show feelings, and then they become afraid to show them. This is too bad.

If kids are adamant about not going to counseling, counseling is not a good idea. Forcing them could cause more problems in the family. Sometimes, if kids realize what the problem is, they can get help in their own way.

There are some times when people should consider getting counseling regardless of what they believe about counseling itself:

When suicide is the next step

When a kid is having a very bad behavioral problem

When kids and parents feel that they can't solve their own problems

When there is no communication at all between parent and child

When a person feels he/she can't cope no matter what has been tried

When a kid or parent is hurting himself/herself with drugs or alcohol

When a kid withdraws

When a kid asks for help

You don't always have to go to a professional counselor to get help with a problem. It is important to go to someone you trust and feel safe with. It could be a priest, minister, rabbi, guidance counselor, an adult friend, parents, or other relatives.

Good friends can often help. Noel said, "Every day you counsel someone even if they only ask you a simple question. One time my best friend's father was threatening to leave home. I tried to help her by just listening to her. Then I told her to try to talk to him. When she did, she found out that he wasn't going to leave, he was only angry." Tina told us about an experience that she had:

"Once I counseled one of my friends. She was feeling down about this guy she was seeing. I just talked to her, but mostly I listened. I think that listening is the best thing you can do for someone who needs help (depending on the situation). Now she comes to me a lot, and I go to her when I need help. So we ended up helping each other."

Counseling can help you get a better perspective on your life. Parents and not just kids can be helped by counseling. Kids notice when a parent is struggling with his or her life. There are times when parents just haven't been able to adjust to the changes in their lives. If you notice this happening to your parent, you might want to suggest that he/she consider talking to somebody. It has to be done carefully so as not to hurt your parent's feelings. The parent might even get mad at you or deny that there is a problem. In that case, don't push the subject; it probably won't do any good. However, certain parents might appreciate the suggestion.

Counseling, to a kid, can seem like, as Julie H. said, "talk, talk, talk." But, as Elizabeth said, "Counseling can be beneficial at times. It can help you think and bring out your true feelings to help you solve your problems." From counseling, you can get new alternatives and suggestions for things. The best thing that can happen is that it can give you someone to talk to who won't judge you or tell anyone. It is important when you go to counseling to tell the truth, if you want someone to be able to help you. Counseling can be good for kids if they think that they want it and feel that they can cope with it. As Tina said, "It can smooth out the bumps in your life but only if you are willing to make a go at it."

DEPRESSION: KIDS

Being depressed is when you are feeling down and not wanted and like nothing is going right for you. You often don't feel like doing anything. You have no energy, you feel tired all the time, and you feel bad about *every* aspect of your life. Maybe you cry all the time. It is a mixture of being sad, lonely, angry, and confused about yourself and possibly others.

When kids are depressed, they think about "all the bad experiences they have had in their lives." Or they think of things like killing themselves *(see* SUICIDE), ways to get revenge on people who have hurt them emotionally, or how lucky everybody else is.

You can tell when you are depressed, as Julie H. said, "if you sit in your room alone a lot just thinking about rotten things, or you walk around silently and slowly all day long." Margae said, "Some kids actually physically feel sick from their mental state." Kids might sleep more than usual, pout, feel self-pity, or yell at people around them. If kids are really depressed, they might not eat.

You know you are *really* depressed when you don't want to see anyone, even your best friend. This mostly occurs when you have talked yourself into thinking that whatever is wrong is all your fault. If this lasts for more than two or three days, it might mean that the depression is getting worse instead of easing.

We think that boys and girls handle being depressed differently. Girls are more likely to get quiet, snappy, or withdrawn. They are usually more emotional. When girls get really upset, they spend a lot of time alone listening to sad songs on the radio or thinking of all the bad times they have had. Boys tend to try to hide it more and pretend that it isn't there. They might get more rowdy, slam things around, and be very grouchy.

A lot of kids who are really sad and are afraid to let it out learn how to act not depressed. They try to hide their awful feelings from the outside world. Kids often do this because they don't want people who care about them to worry. This happens a lot in single-parent families where kids know what a hard time parents are having with all the responsibilities. Elizabeth said, "If you are a good actor, you can smile and laugh on the outside, while on the inside you are crying." If you are depressed, though, as Noel said, "You may get so involved in what you are thinking that you won't hear other people talk to you." But, as Margae said, "Sooner or later, it will show."

Kids in single-parent families get depressed about a number of things. When you think about the missing parent, you might believe, "Dad/Mom isn't here. He/she left because he/she doesn't love me anymore. Why did this have to happen to me?" Not having enough money can make you feel bad, if this is a problem in your family.

Some of us think that kids in single-parent families *do* get depressed more than kids in two-parent families. Missy believes that they have more to think and worry about. Julie H. agreed. She said, "Children in single-parent families get depressed about the normal things, like boy or girl troubles, *plus* the added ones that go along with single-parent living."

Others of us didn't agree. Noel felt that kids in both kinds of families get depressed but for different reasons. She said, "They balance each other out. In two-parent families, kids have to listen to parental fighting, which doesn't go on in single-parent families." And Elizabeth felt that, "Kids are often under more pressure with two parents. They are more strict with kids."

The worst kind of depression is when you feel left out and different from other kids in two-parent families. As Elizabeth said, "Maybe you see other kids with their families and everything looks great for them and nothing looks great for you." You think, "If I only had two parents, then. . . ." This thought comes up at times like school events or teachers' conferences when only one parent is there for you.

The worst things you can do if you get depressed are:

Hide it too long
Push away your friends
Try to kill yourself
Get into drugs
Drink

There are ways to get out of a depression. Julie H. said, "You have to convince yourself that many people have the same or similar problems and that you don't have to carry the burden alone." Margae said, "When I get really down, I try to call up a cheery friend." Elizabeth said, "You can always hope for something great to happen, or you can make something great happen for yourself."

Noel said, "I just talk on the phone or get out of the house for a while. Sometimes I just cry, and then I feel much better." Missy said, "I try to get out and hang out with people my own age and find *something* to do." *(See* FUN.)

When you are in a "total depression" and can't think well, it is important to just do something to keep your mind off the depressing thoughts. You can try to write down or think of all the good things that have happened to you. If you don't do something with it, like tell a friend, write in a diary, or talk to a parent, the depression could become serious and last a long time.

Parents would want to know. They may not know the reason you are feeling down. As Dora said, "If I don't tell my mom, how does she know to do anything about it?" If they yell at you for having a bad attitude, they might not be the best people to talk to. But parents often do things to help kids get over depression like going out to lunch, going to the movies, or just having little chats that make all the difference. They can be good at convincing you that you are loved and that life will go on.

DEPRESSION: PARENTS

Most of the time our parents aren't depressed. We like it that way. When they aren't, they act cheerful, ask us how our day is going, talk about things, joke about things (like spilling milk all over the table), kid us, and let us do things that we want to do.

But *everyone* gets depressed sometimes. As Julie H. said, "Anyone can feel that way. Everyone is human and can hurt sometimes." When a parent does get depressed, it is scary for a kid. Often, parents give kids less love when they are depressed. They sort of shut kids out. Kids look up to parents, and when a parent is depressed, kids feel like the world is coming to an end. Amyee said, "When parents get down, you worry that they might hurt themselves."

It can also make *you* depressed when a parent is sad because the parent's mood affects yours. You feel helpless, and you want your parent to be happy. One girl said, "I hate to see my mother depressed." Or parents' depression can make you mad because parents can get angry looks on their faces and snap at you.

Parents do a lot of the same things that kids do. They seem lonely and confused and like to be by themselves. They can get down about things like money, family problems, a job, or their kids (you). A lot of single parents get upset by kids if they aren't able to control them or if kids are having problems that they don't know how to handle. They can still be upset about the other parent being gone.

Most of us try to do things to get our parents out of a depression. Margae said, "You try to tell them what you have been doing in school to get their minds off the depression." Or you tell jokes and talk about the fun things you have done. It is also a good time to try to be cooperative at home.

Kids often think that it is their fault when a parent is depressed. You imagine that you did something wrong and disappointed your parent. Even if that is true, it is not your fault that a parent is depressed. Remember, they are responsible for their own feelings.

Every parent has a different way of getting out of a depression. Sometimes they just yell at you and that works. Parents can go out or find somebody else with problems to listen to. Or they do things around the house, like clean or fix something.

Most parents make it out of a depression just fine. If you get scared though about your parent, it is okay to talk to close friends and relatives. Try to find someone who knows a lot about your parent's feelings either to get some help for your parent or to ease your fears.

Watching parents live through depression helps kids. You learn things like how people feel when they are depressed, how to handle people when they are depressed, and how to handle yourself when you are depressed. Everyone has to do it differently, but we think that getting out the feeling is the best way to get past a depression because then it is done with.

FUN

Fun is:

Hobbies that are cheap
Changing your room around
Drawing
Painting
Playing baseball
Playing kickball
Having friends over
Going out with a friend
Listening to records
Watching TV
Reading
Joking with brothers and sisters
Joking with a parent
Having a party
Dancing
Cooking something new
Hunting
Window-shopping
Real shopping
Sliding
Skating
Skiing
Going to the movies
Joining a club
Eating
Making something

Going for a walk
Swimming
Roller-skating
Exercising
Talking on the phone!

GETTING INTO TROUBLE

We think of kids who are delinquent as being very disturbed. Most likely they have had bad home lives and have gotten into the wrong crowd and broken the law a lot. Sometimes, but not always, they have come from bad neighborhoods where they grew up surrounded by other troubled kids. They experience a lot of peer pressure to become delinquent; they feel pushed by their friends and decide that they have to do it. Sometimes kids who are delinquent are bad people. Most of the time, we think they are good people who make big mistakes. We think that many, as Julie H. said, "just got rotten breaks when they were younger."

Delinquent things kids do are:

Stealing
Vandalism
Mugging
Drinking
Using drugs

There are a lot of reasons why kids decide to become delinquent. When kids use drugs and alcohol, they are more likely to get into trouble because they do things without thinking. Some kids get into trouble out of curiosity or boredom. They just want to see how much they can get away with. Most kids who get into trouble do it as a way to feel important. Some were raised in families where everybody got into trouble and just don't know any differently. Some do it as a way to get revenge or to get attention. You want to get back at a parent for something done to you, like being punished or abandoned. Maybe a parent is alcoholic *(see* ALCOHOL) or abusive *(see* CHILD ABUSE). Maybe a parent is too close or too distant. Or you want to prove to a parent, "I run my life, not you."

Some people think that *all* kids who live in single-parent families become delinquent. It gets drilled into their heads that kids in single-parent families are bad and don't get brought up right. Kids who are delinquent can come from *any* kind of family.

We do think though that there are things about living in single-parent families that can help to push a kid into acting delinquent. Anthony Krulikowski, our vice-principal, taught in a program for delinquent kids for ten years. He said, "Single-parent families aren't the cause of delinquency, but if you check the backgrounds of those kids who are delinquent, many of them come from single-parent homes." It is true that there *can* be more problems to face. Kids *might* have more frustrations (depends on the family). It could be harder to get the attention that they want. They could have more fears and anger. Mark Denton told us his thoughts about kids from single-parent families and delinquency: "I think my living in a single-parent family had a big effect on my getting into trouble. I was living with my mother and running wild. She had no control over me whatsoever. It was okay, actually, until my mom got her boyfriend. Before that, the kids were everything to her. But when her boyfriend came on the scene, it was different. We took a back seat to him. I was so jealous and angry that I couldn't control it. I figured that if nobody gave a damn, I might as well just get into trouble. I know a lot of kids in single-parent families who have gotten into trouble, and this is a common way it happens."

Being delinquent is complicated. You can have a lot of different feelings about it. When you start getting into trouble, you find yourself in disbelief. It is a shock to you, and you didn't realize that what you were doing was that serious. You feel bad, embarrassed, and ashamed. Often, you feel angry that you are ruining your life.

The problem is that once you become delinquent, it can be hard to stop. You usually feel a sense of belonging when you get into trouble, that you are just like your friends. This makes you feel important. If you have a low opinion of yourself, you might even be proud that you are good at something. You might think that you are "cool." If you get your name in the papers, your friends might be in awe, and you feel famous.

All of us, boys included, think that boys are more likely to become delinquent than girls. Plenty of girls become delinquent, but boys have a macho image to live up to. It can be harder for them to turn down a dare.

There are exciting parts about being delinquent that also make it hard to give up. There is a thrill to the danger and knowledge that you are doing something wrong and not getting caught. You can start to think, as Julie H. said, "that you are big and tough and that nothing can hurt you." Usually, you get a lot of attention (see ATTENTION). Plus, once people start thinking that you are bad and calling you a "delinquent," you decide that if you are labeled that way, you should behave that way. As Noel said, "You have a name to live up to."

When there is someone in the family who is delinquent, the rest of the family gets affected. If you are the oldest, younger brothers and sisters might look up to you and try out getting in trouble, too. It can cause parents, together or divorced, to fight. It can be devastating and break a family apart. The good thing is that sometimes it can do just the opposite and bring the family closer together (see COUNSELING), hopefully including the kid who is getting into trouble.

Kids who are delinquent can straighten out. Some just need a parent or a stepparent, someone who cares, to talk to them. Mr. Krulikowski said, "I have seen it time and time again. Once a family gets stabilized, the delinquency begins to end." Counseling, if the kid will go, can help sometimes, too (see COUNSELING). Or just getting arrested once can do the trick for a lot of kids. Mark also told us: "I had slashed some tires on a car in town. I was staying with my grandmother at the time. The police came to my grandmother's door and said that they knew I had done it, and I could confess to them or to my grandmother if that would be easier. I was scared. Looking back, I could have lied and maybe gotten out of it, but I was so scared that I told the truth. I thought about what might happen to me—going to court, kissing the town goodbye for five or six years, and going to jail. I imagined getting taken into a system that didn't care about me at all and being treated like just another crook. I was really humbled for a long time."

Other kids get scared when they do something awful, like hurt someone very badly. This scares them into changing. There are private schools or treatment centers where kids can go if their delinquency is getting very serious. In these centers, groups of kids help each other to not get into trouble.

Trying to understand delinquents is important. They should be treated as if everyone makes mistakes. They should be helped to understand *why* they did the things that they did. It is important that they be listened to. Some kids just desperately need to feel understood.

We don't think they should get too much sympathy though. It is important that they know that what they have done is *wrong*. It is important to be *firm*. You have got to mean business, or some kids will take advantage of your understanding. Everybody should know that they have to answer for their actions.

GRANDPARENTS

Since getting into a single-parent family, many of us have gotten closer to our grandparents. We see them more often than when we were in a two-parent family. A lot of us live really close to at least one set of our grandparents. According to Mr. David Mellinger, a specialist in gerontology at United Counseling Service, most older people live in close distance to at least some of their grandchildren even though families are spreading out more and more.

Grandparents are very important to kids who live in single-parent families. Many grandparents provide kids with the moral support they need to deal with all the changes that take place.

Noel said, "They help you if you get in an argument with your mom or dad. They listen to problems that you can't talk to your parent about." Tom said, "You can talk to them about things that could embarrass or hurt your parent. You can entrust them with secrets, as long as they aren't too big." As Amyee said, "When my mom is working, we just go over to their house if we need someone to talk to or to be with."

In single-parent families, grandparents help in raising you. They protect you and offer advice. They even lecture you on your behavior when it is bad and discipline you (see RULES AT HOME). Missy said, "They tell you what to do and where to go and can yell at you just like a parent." Amyee said, "They do everything like a parent would, and sometimes they are even there *more* often." A lot of grandparents let kids stay with them for periods of time. Stephen said, "My grandmother lets me stay there whenever I want to."

A lot of our grandparents cared for us when our parents were having a hard time. And they still offer comfort to us and our parents. Sheri said, "My grandmother has been there when my mom didn't have anyone else to help her." Noel said, "One time my grandparents told me to give my mom a chance because single parents have a lot more to deal with alone. They said that when she gets grouchy, just try." Elizabeth said, "My grandmother grew up in a single-parent family. She said that the remaining parent has a double job to do and that means that kids should try extra hard to help out." Amyee said, "My grandparents would do anything for any of us."

Sometimes they can take on the job of *being* the other parent. Noel said, "I have gotten close to my grandfather. He is like a father to me, and when my mom is busy, he is always there." Or let's say that you live with your mother, your grandfather can offer you advice much the way a father would.

This doesn't mean that we think grandparents should live with us. As much as we love our grandparents, we don't think it is a good idea. One girl said, "I like the idea of them living close but not us living all together. I would probably get sick of them and they would get sick of me and then we would slip away from each other." If grandparents lived with you, the job of parenting could get all confused. The kid could end up not knowing *who* to listen to if there is disagreement. It would be easy for there to be a lot of fighting over the kids.

An exception would be if they were very sick or very lonely and without any money at all. And, of course, it depends on the family. We just think that they should live their own lives (and us ours). Everyone needs privacy. The more people who live together, the grouchier everyone can get.

Sometimes kids don't see the grandparents who were the parents of the missing parent as often as when that parent was around. Also, kids who were young when a parent disappeared or died may have never met that set of grandparents. This is hard on kids. They often think that grandparents who don't see them don't care about them.

As Elizabeth said, "The grandchildren might be the light of their life." Missy said, "My grandmother favors my brother, sister, and me because we were her son's children, and she loved him a lot." Noel added, "A child has a special relationship with grandparents, and no one has the right to take that away."

We think grandparents have a right to see their grandchildren as often as they like because they are a part of the family. Grandparents can get upset if they don't see their grandchildren. They might think that their grandchildren are angry with them or don't like them. One girl told us, "My grandma and grampa (my dad's mom and dad) get very sad because they don't see us more. We are now trying to see them more, especially since my grampa is dying."

There are a lot of grandparents now, according to Mr. Mellinger, who care enough about their grandchildren that they are taking it to court. He said, "Legislators are trying to implement a 'grandparents' visitation rights' law in Vermont. This law would give grandparents the right to see a child even if the parent doesn't care or have visitation rights."

We think that grandparents should have visitation rights, if that is necessary, as a way to maintain contact. As Julie H. said, "Visiting will differ with each case. Some will want to be together all the time whereas others may not." Even if grandparents live far away, it is important to have a relationship with them. It can be hard, but you can do it. You can always write or call or visit on vacations. The only way it is impossible is if your grandparents refuse to make contact with you.

Having grandparents who are involved with us makes us feel good. Stephen said, "It makes me feel like I have somebody to talk to and relate to." It can give you hope for yourself. Noel said, "If they are together, it makes you feel like marriage can work, and just because your parents aren't together doesn't mean that your marriage will fail."

You always know, too, that somebody will be there for you if something awful happens in your family. You can often go to your grandparents and get from them things that your parents won't give you (they spoil us to an extent). And we feel good being able to give to them. As Amyee said, "They need someone there for them as well."

Kids who don't see their grandparents (either set) are missing a lot. According to Missy, "They give you a great deal of love. When people get older, they take things to heart in a way that they didn't when they were younger." Sheri said, "You would miss fun, goodies, love, and getting spoiled (I read somewhere that if your mother says no, ask your grandmother!)."

Grandparents can be great friends. Elizabeth said, "Every Christmas my grandma and I go shopping and out to supper. My grandmother is really terrific. She has *character*. We get laughing so hard that we can't stop. And that is so much fun!" You miss special things you would have done with them. Amyee said, "Last summer they invited us to go on a camping trip to a lake for three days. My mother stayed home. My grandparents taught us how to do things in the water off a diving board and went on bike trips with us and did a lot of other stuff. It was really fun."

Kids lose out on getting to know a whole side of their family and a link to their family's past. To a kid, it can feel just like not having your parents. Kids lose out on the chance to get different adults' viewpoints and advice. As Stephen said, "Grandparents just have a lot to share." Missy said, "My grandmother always tells me things about my father and how good he was. She told me lots of funny things that he did when he was young."

Our grandparents have taught us so much. Stephen said, "Through my grandmother, I have learned to enjoy life while I can." Noel said, "I know now that life can be whatever I make it to be. It has made a difference because now I try to help out more." Sheri said, "My grandmother has taught me that I don't know everything about life, and it is okay to be myself." The most important thing we have learned is that you can take many blows in life, but it still goes on. It is more important to live with your problems rather than dwell on them.

HOLIDAYS

A lot of kids in single-parent families spend holidays like Christmas and Easter at the house of the parent who doesn't have custody of them. In some families, the holidays are split between the two parents' houses. Tom said, "My brother and sister and I go back and forth between my mom's and my dad's house on the day of the holiday. We usually end up having two or three dinners. It is fun, no problem."

If you live in a single-parent family because of the death of a parent or abandonment by a parent, holidays aren't always so much fun. One girl told us, "Holidays in these kinds of families rot! Especially when the parent you live with has to work. You get used to peanut butter and jelly sandwiches on Christmas and chicken noodle soup on Thanksgiving. On Christmas, you either have to get up really early to open your presents or you have to wait until late that night." A lot of kids who we know in these situations go to relatives' or grandparents' houses for holidays.

But holidays in a single-parent family don't have to be any

different from in a two-parent family. Missy said, "It seems the same to me. Every holiday, my mother, my brothers, my sister, and all our relatives get together. I think all holidays are *great* with or without two parents."

IN THE PAST

One thing that we wondered about was whether or not living in single-parent families in the past was the same as living in them now. Ms. Sweeney said, "It was not as common years ago to divorce as it is now. Death of a parent was more likely the way to get into a single-parent family. It was much harder for kids back then. There wasn't as much help for kids so they had to handle it themselves."

We thought the best way to get some idea of what it was like to live in a single-parent family in the past was to ask adults who grew up in one. Elizabeth's grandmother, Catherine Dermody, talked to us about what her life was like after her father's death. "I think, looking back, that survival was the greatest thing, just keeping going. My mom did not take a job. She was from a farm family. Her work all her life was housework. She made and did everything herself. Everybody in the family contributed to keeping things going. I went to work when I was thirteen years old by putting my hair up to make myself look older. I worked in a store and would put prices on paper bags, then add them up.

"My older brother was a male image for me. My mom relied on him to keep me in line, and I resented it. For example, if my brother was supposed to pick me up at the dance, I would leave early to be spared the embarrassment of being picked up by him.

"I didn't know many other kids who lived in single-parent families, maybe just two or three. I was never treated differently by kids who lived with both of their parents. We didn't dwell on the psychological aspects of life. We would go along and do what our parent expected of us. Life was simpler then. I was never resentful of my father's death. You just didn't raise as many questions as young people do today. Life is different now for kids. There is a more difficult and more advanced quality of living. I am not sure that we have done them any favors. They feel questions and problems that we just didn't have.

"I do think that my older brother and sister were more affected than I was because of the ages they were when my father died. My brother had to take on more responsibility in our family, and my sister was not able to go to school; she was very bright.

"But we weren't as demanding. There was never the competition that there is today as far as clothing and possessions. We were a more homogenous group, and there was not as much peer pressure. We never thought, 'We are poor and can't afford something.' If you wanted something, you earned it; if you couldn't have it, you couldn't.

"My mom was forty-two when my father died. She never dated. She felt, 'I had the best, I don't want the rest.' There were also men who stayed single the rest of their lives. Often, if men lost their wives, there was a maiden sister who would step in to help out. Women were good at coping. I don't think they are more capable than men, but I think they are more adaptable.

"I had a very independent mother who would let me make my own decisions. My mom and I got along very well. She gave me things like piano lessons and required me to do well and behave. I believe that kids rise to expectations and that the more you demand of them, the more they are capable of.

"Knowing my mom and the things that she did, she had to truly sacrifice. I liked my independence as much as she did. My mother took very little for herself. There was much less competition between parents and children to 'find yourself.' I think that nowadays parents don't let kids be children long enough. My mother was remarkable. She did well for a country girl with little education."

Our principal, Mrs. Rudd, came from a single-parent family through a divorce, but not as long ago as Elizabeth's grandmother. Her parents divorced at a time when divorce didn't happen as much as it does today. She told us about her thoughts and feelings. "I guess that I didn't know what was going on when my parents divorced. Maybe I don't remember much because I suppressed it. When I was growing up, you were really different if you didn't have both parents in the home. So I did realize that I felt unique in that respect. It felt like I was the only one who didn't have two parents at home, and everyone else did. I felt like it set me apart. I never talked to friends about the divorce when I was younger. I kept it to myself. Most all my friends lived with both of their parents. It is different now. I would guess that approximately forty percent of the kids in the junior high in our town live or have lived in a single-parent family.

"My mother worked, and I spent a lot of time alone even when they were married. That didn't change when my parents got a divorce. Money became a problem, though. At least my mother thought it was. She lived on alimony, and I know she had trouble making ends meet. I can't say that I ever felt it was a problem.

"I got a lot of attention from both of my parents. They lived near each other so I could live with either one. Both of them were vying for my affection so they lavished quite a bit of attention on me. My parents were friendly. It was basically a friendly divorce, and we always would get together for the holidays.

"I think I would have liked it better to have both parents together all the time, but I don't remember thinking the thought of how nice it probably would have been. I do know that I was scared about marriage. I figured that when I got married I was going to make it work. I have been married for twenty-seven years."

JOINT CUSTODY

Joint custody is when two divorced parents share custody of you. It is a legal term that means both parents have the right to make decisions that affect your life. If it works well, it means that both parents take part in raising you.

Joint custody is getting a lot of attention nowadays. Scott said, "More people are trying joint custody. There are mixed feelings about it. Some people think it is great, some think it doesn't work at all." We think that the biggest reason joint custody is being considered more often is that both mothers and fathers are realizing how much they love and want to be an active part of their kids' lives.

In the past, mothers almost always got custody of the children. Today, fathers are seeking custody of their children more often and getting increasing legal rights from the court. Women now see themselves not only as mothers but also as people with careers. Margae said, "I know a family where the children live with the father in their own home. The mother goes to college and is getting a degree so she can work and support herself and the kids later. She visits them on weekends and her vacations. When she finishes school, they will switch." Your parents make the decision to have joint custody, but the court has to say it is okay. Michelle said, "My cousin, who worked for a lawyer, said it is kind of easy. If both parents agree and have a good plan, a judge almost always approves it." In allowing joint custody, we think that judges should be sure both parents are fit to care for the kids, have a good custody agreement with one another, and provide suitable living arrangements for everybody. The most important thing is that parents *want* to care for the kids.

In order for joint custody to work, parents have to learn to get along for the kids' sake. There are a lot of special details that go into joint custody so, as Elizabeth said, "parents need to have good communication and respect for each other." Amyee said, "They have to not *hate* each other. They need to both love the kids enough to understand what they want and need."

Often parents set up the joint custody arrangement in a way that means both parents are allowed to spend equal time with the kids. A kid may spend six months with one parent and the next six months with the other parent. Michelle has a friend who "lives in Bennington with her father. Her mom lives in Omaha, Nebraska. She goes with her mom every summer and every other Christmas. She has lived with her dad for three years, and the next year she is going to live with her mom for a couple of years." It can be shorter periods of time as well. Dora goes back and forth between her mother's and her father's house every two weeks.

Spending equal time with both parents can be attractive to kids. It provides kids with different life experiences because of living large blocks of time in different places. If there was a good agreement between parents, it can stop the fighting over the kid that often takes place when parents divorce.

But joint custody doesn't mean that you must have equal amounts of time at both houses. Chris and Matt's parents have no set arrangement. The boys go back and forth between their parents' houses whenever they want. They make the arrangements themselves. It is also possible to live with your mother and visit your father on weekends or the other way around. Your parents could still have joint custody of you.

This is important because kids don't always want equal amounts of time with each of their parents. One girl said, "I want more time with my mom because she and I are a little closer than my dad and I are." Elizabeth said, "I wouldn't like equal time. I like having one home base. I would choose to visit the other parent more often, but I would stay at one house most of the time."

We know that joint custody is not a magic answer to divorce or separation. As Elizabeth said, "Reality is always there. There will always be some complaint or some gripe. No one is ever completely satisfied; that is just human nature."

Even if you want joint custody, there are always problems that go along with it. You may have to get used to stepparents or live-in friends. There is often disagreement over time with one parent or the other, regardless of the court agreement. Transportation is a problem. If the parents live far away from each other, who pays the airfare? Plus, it can be hard to uproot every so often for any reason. And what if parents, even after the best of agreements, just stop talking to each other? It can put a lot of responsibility on kids to make important decisions.

Joint custody doesn't work for every family or for every kid. Some kids don't like one parent and don't particularly want to be with that parent so much, especially if the parent is alcoholic or has been abusive to them or their other parent in the past. Also, as Scott said, "Joint custody could mean that you would have two parents tugging at you from two different sides at once."

If joint custody meant that the kid had to go far away to live, as Elizabeth said, "It would be hard for him or her to leave friends for long periods of time. It may mean, too, that you would have to change schools and get used to another one. Sometimes, you just wouldn't want to leave the parent you are with."

But we do have fantasies of joint custody situations that include important parts from a kid's point of view and could improve kids' lives:

> Having two houses connected by a garage. Anytime you wanted to see the other parent, you could go next door, and there wouldn't be any problems.

> Every month you go to a different house. If you had a brother or a sister, you could switch so each of you could be alone sometimes and together sometimes. Your parents would live in the same area and would be friends. Each one is fair—not too spoiling and not too strict. You would go to the same school and see your same friends.

> Your dad lives around the block. Your mom has you for six months, and you see your dad every other weekend. Then you switch and do it the other way. You keep the same friends. You have a dog and a gerbil at your dad's and a cat and a fish at your mom's. All the stuff you need is at both houses.

Kids sometimes prefer joint custody situations. Having joint custody can take some of the pressure off single parents. Sheri said, "This way parents would get to see their kids and then get a rest." Parents wouldn't have to have the responsibility of being a parent all the time. They would get free time for themselves, making them happier parents and you a happier kid.

We think that joint custody could help kids adjust to the loss of the family as it was and still have a good upbringing. It can allow kids to feel cared for by both parents. As Sheri said, "It means that, if kids love each parent, they won't miss one because they had to live with the other." Kids like joint custody when they love both parents equally and don't want to have to choose between them just because their parents are divorcing.

KIDNAPPING

Nowadays, being kidnapped by the other parent comes into kids' minds a lot. Some kids even wish that they would be kidnapped. One fourteen-year-old girl said, "Being kidnapped would be great, just wonderful. Then I could live with my dad." Kids have these thoughts whenever they are having a hard time living with the parent who has custody of them. Maybe they feel they are being mistreated by that parent. Or it could be that they just miss living with the other parent.

Most kids fear it. One girl said, "Before my dad went to jail, he would pick me up. We would go for long rides and talk. I was always afraid that he would keep me. I wasn't concerned that he would hurt me. I just thought that we wouldn't go back." Another girl said, "I am the oldest. I get scared about my brother and sister when they go to visit with my dad. Every time they go, I worry that he might keep them."

We aren't sure whether to call being taken by another parent "kidnapping" or not. Julie H. said, "If the parent takes an unwilling child out of a town or state, that is kidnapping." Michelle added, "It is kidnapping, too, if a parent just does not let the other parent see the kid even if they live in the same town or state." No matter what you call it, kids have fears when it happens. Fears like:

How will I get away?

What is going to happen to me?

Will I ever see my other parent again?

Will I be hurt?

How will my parent at home handle it?

We don't think that kids have a lot of control over whether they can get kidnapped or not. You could have some control if you were old enough to fight back or to talk the parent out of it when it is happening. You could try to run away, but, if you don't know where you are, this could be a bad decision. Getting to a phone to call the other parent might work if you get a chance. However, you might be so confused about your feelings that you don't know what to do.

The only thing you might be able to do is to reason with your parent. Let them know that it is not what you want. Tina said, "You could talk very seriously to the parent and say, 'This isn't right, and you know it. I don't want to go so why are we doing this?' You would want to talk to them calmly so that you could get them to take you back in a way that nothing would come of it." You could tell them you will talk it over with your parent and try to work everything out. But we think that doing any of these things would be hard, regardless of how old you are.

One reason that it might be hard for a kid to have any control over being kidnapped is that it happens in a way that isn't unusual. We think kids might be likely to feel the tension but not be quite sure what it means. A parent could pick you up and say, "We will be back home soon," and then you just don't go back. One boy told us, "One time my dad said that we were going to be working on the car. We drove off and went across the state line into New Hampshire. I didn't want to go, but there was nothing I could do."

Some kidnappings are more dramatic. Elizabeth said, "A girl was picked up from school by her father. Her mom and dad were divorced, and it was a hard one. The girl wasn't heard of again for about four or five years when her picture was in a paper for winning something in a contest. The detectives working on the case saw the picture. By the time they went to the town, she was gone. About two more years passed. They discovered what school she was in by another picture and finally found her. Her father went to prison, and the mother and daughter were reunited."

Michelle said, "One of my sister's friends had gotten a divorce. One day she came home from work, and her apartment was empty. The babysitter was gone and so was her little girl. The sitter had left a note saying that the little girl's father had come and taken her for ice cream. She went over to her ex-husband's apartment, and his roommate told her that he had said he was going to Virginia. She spent a long time searching for her daughter, found her, and pressed charges against her ex-husband."

We think that things usually lead up to a kidnapping by a parent. Sometimes the parent who has the kids is abusing them, and the other parent just comes and takes them away. If either parent is alcoholic, this would increase the chances, too. Many times one parent just thinks the kids would be better off with that parent.

The most common thing that can cause a kidnapping is hatred between parents. One parent will be using the kid to hurt the other parent. A lot of times one parent could be keeping the other parent from seeing the kids. Often, there is a lot of bitterness over the custody of the children. Let's say the parent with custody moves far away and makes it impossible for the parent to see them.

As Tina said, "If a parent doesn't have any visiting rights, he or she may be feeling desperate. I think that a parent has to be pretty desperate if they kidnap their child." As Elizabeth said, "When a parent doesn't see a child for a long time, he or she might just get the urge to do something rash."

The only ways we know to avoid kidnapping are for parents to work out their differences or for kids to try to see both parents enough so that neither feels neglected. If you can't visit, call or write to the other parent to avoid having that parent feel so desperate.

Kids should know:

That kidnapping can happen

Why parents would do it

Not to let themselves be bribed by a parent
How not to panic
How to talk to a parent about it
To be cautious about seeing angry parents alone

Whether or not a parent should be punished by the law for taking a child really depends on the situation. It should depend on things like how far did they go, how long were they gone, and did the kid resist? If the reason that the parent kidnapped the kid is because he or she wasn't being allowed to see the child, then punishment might not be right, especially if the parent was doing it for love and not for money or the thrill of it. If a child was really being abused and the law wasn't helping the parent to get the child away from the abusing parent, the parent who takes the kid shouldn't be punished.

We think that kidnapping is wrong because it involves force and ends up hurting everyone. We can understand a parent's feelings about wanting to kidnap; we don't think it is fair for a parent never to see a child. But parents need to know that, no matter how much a kid loved the parent who took him/her, we think that the kid couldn't help but feel resentful, sad, and distrustful about that parent. Kidnapping just causes too much heartbreak.

KIDS AND FUNERALS

Funerals are scary for kids. You imagine chairs, flowers, an organ, darkness, dead people, and relatives hovering over you. It is like someday you are going to die, and everybody you know is going to be crying about you. When you go to a funeral, you get, as Laura said, "butterflies in your stomach like when you do something for the first time." Missy said, "You imagine yourself crying before you even get there." It is strange.

There is so much crying that you just get an awful feeling. One girl said, "Everyone was looking at my dad; it was spooky. I had this feeling of being dead and buried myself." You watch your other parent crying, and you start to think of all the things that you should have done differently. You feel so guilty.

Most funerals last about an hour. There are usually a lot of prayers, and people announce what they felt about the person. A lot of times they have a service at maybe a church and then again when they put the person in the ground. Afterward, everybody goes to your house. From a kid's point of view, this makes you feel bad. We think that people make too much of it all.

Parents should talk to kids about funerals. We think that the more kids know before the funeral, the less they will be afraid. They should warn kids about all the crying and that everybody will feel sorry for them. Kids don't like people to feel sorry for them because it makes them feel helpless, and they don't like feeling that way.

Parents usually understand about kids and funerals. But some parents try to force kids into doing things they think *ought* to be done which are uncomfortable for kids. It can be really hard, and some kids just can't take it. We think that kids should have a choice as to whether to go to the funeral or not. Often, if given a choice, kids will decide to go on their own anyway. Debby said, "I wanted to go because it was the last time I would see any trace of him forever. I had to see him off."

There are benefits if you decide to go to the funeral. You get to see who cares for your parent and hear what people have thought about him/her. Bronwen told us, "All of us went to the funeral. There was a finality to it. We thought, 'Now this is real.' It snapped us out of the daze after my mother's death."

Also, funerals can be happy events. Some people don't want friends and relatives to be sad when they go. They want them to remember the good things. One girl said, "Everyone was happy at my grandmother's funeral. I couldn't believe it. I asked my mother, and she said that my grandmother would have wanted it that way."

MONEY

Money is something that you trade for an object or a service (and causes a lot of people to go buggy). To kids, it is, as Margae said, "Thin green stuff that gets us what we want and is really essential. Most times it is hard to get, and it spends really fast." Nowadays, you want money for things like junk food, music, new clothes, and a lot of things that you could do without for the time being if you really thought about it.

When you have money, you feel "high and mighty." You think about everything that you can buy with it. Missy said, "I get excited because I can go out and buy new clothes or whatever I want." And when you can go out and buy what you want, it makes the value of what you are buying seem greater, even if it only costs twenty-five cents.

When you don't have much money, you feel like a grub! You walk around thinking, "I can't afford this or I can't afford that because I don't have enough money." When you know that money at home is tight, you don't ask for things like ice cream or the "neat shirt" at the department store. If you want to go to the movies with a friend and your parent says, "We have to pay the rent," you feel frustrated and angry.

The hardest thing that often happens to kids in single-parent families is that you go from having enough money to not having as much. This often happens for a while when parents divorce or when a parent dies with no insurance. It can be frustrating because you are used to getting certain things and then you have to get used to not being able to have them.

Kids can feel desperate about money. As Margae said, "Money is the key in this country"—Missy added, "In the world"—"and it determines your social status. Money decides what you eat, where you live, what you do—really everything. Not being able to afford something you want makes you feel rotten."

Some families go from not having much to having a lot if a

parent died and left insurance. This can have its problems, too, because you can start to overspend. Also, the money doesn't always make a difference to the kid. One girl said, "I am not happy about having more money because my father is dead."

We think that every kid should learn about money. As Julie H. said, "Money problems aren't limited to kids in single-parent families." Margae added, "Knowing how to manage money is important to everyone, but a kid from a single-parent family is more likely to need to learn sooner and more efficiently." We think it is important that kids learn the cost of the necessities like:

Groceries
Fuel
Medical expenses
Utilities (light, heat, phone)
Clothing
Rent or mortgage
Cars

Even though we think, as Julie H. said, "that deep down, rich kids, poor kids, middle-class kids are all the same," having money raises your prestige. Being a "rich kid" or a "poor kid" can make a difference in how you feel about yourself. Some of it depends on the individual, but often a kid who has money will look down on a kid who doesn't have as much. It is as though the kid weren't good enough. And kids who don't have as much money will look at kids who are well off and stereotype them as being "snobs."

Your life experience is different, too. Kids in families with little money have to work harder to get the things they want. They have to go out and get odd jobs. Kids who have money get a lot of the "extras" of life but often miss out on the things that having to work for money can teach. When you don't have as much, you learn to cherish what you have.

One thing that we are sure of is that having money doesn't mean that you don't have problems. Sometimes you may even have more. When you have a lot of something, a certain responsibility goes along with it. Having a great deal of money can also mean that you get frustrated easier when you don't get what you want.

Almost everybody fights about money whether or not they have a lot or a little. It could be that there isn't enough money, and people fight because they can't pay the bills. They get frustrated and take it out on someone else. Some families have plenty of money but argue about what to spend it on. As Julie H. said, "Money has a weird effect on people. Deep down everybody wants more, more, more."

We agree with Tom, who said, "Money isn't everything." There are plenty of situations where people are rich and unhappy and other people are poor and happy. On the other hand, we know what Elizabeth meant when she said, "I would like a real-life experience on what to do with a lot of money!"

PETS AND US

When you have a pet, you can learn a lot about yourself and others. You can talk to your animals, and they can't talk back (but they can walk off). Through them you can learn how to talk to yourself in a useful way. These are some of the things our pets have taught us:

When I get mad at my mom, brother, or sister, I go and talk to my dog. He never blames me for anything, and through talking to him I get the answers I need for myself. I can solve my own problems with a little help from someone who will listen and not say anything.

When I get really lonely or scared, I use my dog sort of like a "security blanket." I have learned that I need someone more than I'd like to admit sometimes.

When I'm feeling down and I need to have someone with me to feel sorry for me, I go to my dog and say, "You are

who cares for me, nobody else cares." He gives
and starts whining. It makes me feel good that
res.

when I'm mad at my parents I will scream and
yell out all the things I would like to say to them at my cat.
She just listens, and by saying those things out loud, I can
usually see how dumb or not so dumb my complaints are.

I was coming back from California, and I just had found
out that my parents were getting a divorce. I took my cats
and went up to my room and played with them.

RULES AT HOME

In single-parent families, one parent at a time has all the responsibility for discipline. Discipline at home means rules. Rules
are a help to kids so that they know what they are supposed to do to
stay out of trouble. We think that everybody needs rules—boys and
girls, kids in single-parent families, and kids in two-parent families.
When parents discipline kids, they tell them how to do things and
help them if they don't understand. Scott said, "Good discipline is
designed to prevent problems. It is teaching what is right and
wrong."

Most single parents have to adjust to disciplining kids by
themselves. It can take a long time for some, especially if the other
parent enforced most of the rules. Parents are usually able to manage well after a period of trial and error even though it is never easy.
Tom said, "My mother sets the rules. She learned very fast. We
have a lot of rules, and they work (most of the time). The important thing is that once a rule has been set it gets enforced." Julie B.
said, "My mother has been disciplining us for a long time. She has
done a pretty good job by herself." Or Missy said, "For my mom, it
came naturally. Sometimes I wish it had taken longer."

Some parents like doing all the disciplining by themselves. It
means, for them, not having to argue with other parents who dis-

agree with rules they have set. But it can be lonely, too. It is hard to always have to be "the mean one." This parent has to carry all the guilt, too, if he/she is wrong or hits you for something. The parent out of the house often gets to look like "the saint." Although we think that, as Julie B. said, "if you have done something really bad, parents can call one another to help out."

One thing that happens in single-parent families is that parents' boyfriends or girlfriends get involved in disciplining kids. We don't like this. A girl said, "A boyfriend and girlfriend should not get involved in disciplining. That makes a kid *hate* that person. When my mom had a boyfriend, he used to try to discipline us. He would make us say 'Please' or 'Excuse me' when we left the dinner table." We hated him for that—we *hated* that. I think my mother knew. She tried to get him not to do that. She would say, 'They are my kids, I can do it myself.' But he kept on doing it."

A boyfriend or girlfriend being involved only makes things more complicated. Kids are usually jealous anyhow because he/she is getting attention that they want. We just think that the friend isn't part of the family, and unless the kids are doing something drastically wrong, it doesn't work very well.

Discipline is different from punishment. Tom said, "Punishment is what happens to you after you break the rules." Punishment is the action taken after somebody has done something he/she knows is wrong. These are some kinds of punishment that all kids get:

Being grounded

Having privileges taken away

Getting yelled at

As Norman said, "Sometimes punishment is good." The best kind of punishment for kids is when they learn a lesson about what to do the next time they get into the situation.

SUICIDE

Suicide is, as Amyee said, "when you get sick of life or people and kill yourself." People commit suicide to escape problems and responsibilities. Some people have just lost the will to live. Others commit suicide to avoid pain, like if they have cancer and know that they are going to die and just don't want to go through it.

A lot of us know kids in single-parent families and two-parent families who have tried to commit suicide. They have done it for a lot of different reasons. Some feel that they have too many responsibilities and are under stress and pressure. They start to think that they just can't handle it. Some get upset by school-related things like getting into arguments with friends or feeling shunned. Other kids are afraid of failure.

Elizabeth said, "Some kids feel that they aren't needed or wanted." They feel that parents don't understand them, or they get upset because parents are away so much at work. There are also many young parents who weren't ready for kids in the first place but had them anyway. Other kids have no will to live because they had something bad happen to them. They often think of killing themselves if a loved one dies, and they want to be with that person.

Kids are more likely to try to hurt themselves if they are drinking or taking other drugs. It takes away some of their self-control, especially when they drink and drive. Michelle said, "Drugs and alcohol get kids so messed up that they can't take it anymore. Then they put themselves out of their misery."

Adults, not just kids, commit suicide (or try). We worry about kids with a parent who tried to or did kill himself/herself. We think a kid is more likely to try it then, too. One girl we interviewed said, "When my uncle killed himself, he sent my aunt away with the kids for the weekend. He didn't do anything that weekend. When she came back home, they went to bed. My aunt woke up the next morning and felt that something was wrong. My uncle usually went out for an early morning walk, but that morning she was worried. She was going to send the kids to look for him but decided to go herself. She went out back and saw him hanging from a tree. He didn't leave a note. He was a quiet guy. I worry about what will happen to the family."

Sometimes kids use suicide just as a way to get attention or as a way to hurt somebody they are mad at. One girl told us, "I know a kid who lives with both of her parents. Her mom is always yelling at her. One night she called me and said, 'I'm going to do it, this time I'm going to do it. I just took a lot of aspirin.' Earlier that night, she had made me leave the house because she and her mom were having a big fight. She called me about midnight. I ran down to her house in the pitch dark. She was lying on her bed, and I thought she was dead. 'Are you okay?' I asked. She answered, 'Yes, I'm just asleep.' I read the label on the bottle and found out that eight aspirin was the maximum you could take and still be okay. Later, we got into a big fight over it. I told her that she just wanted to scare everyone. I was so mad."

When you think about killing yourself, you usually decide that no one likes you and that your parents don't want you around and that it will be better for everyone if you just aren't there. As Michelle said, "You feel like the situation has reached an extreme. You start thinking only about yourself and not the people you will leave behind." When you get to this point, little things can tip you over the edge. Amyee said, "Like if your mom yells at you, that means she doesn't want you. If she doesn't want you, then who would?" A lot of thoughts go through your head. As Darcey said, "How much your friends will miss you when you are gone." When you are thinking about hurting yourself, you wonder, "Who will be crying at my funeral?"

Suicide is a selfish thing to do. One girl said, "I know a girl who committed suicide. Her parents and their close friends were so hurt. To think that she blew her brains out in her own home. Not only did she deny herself the right to live but she also denied her parents the right to watch her grow up. I think she did it as an easy way out of life's problems, but she forgot that there were joys in life, too."

We think that often kids know when another kid might try to commit suicide before a parent does. Kids spend more time around each other and can tell when someone is really down or withdrawn. Julie B. said, "A lot of times you pick out things in your friends that make you worry." They hear each other talk about angry thoughts. For example, one of our sisters was at a party once where a guy came up to her and whispered something to her. She worried about it. Later they found him upstairs slitting his wrist. She felt terrible.

There are some things that you should know about suicide:

There is help. Most people who commit suicide don't mean to do it. It is a plea for help: "Does someone care enough about me to stop me?" Someone usually cares, but often people don't realize it in time.

If you really think that a friend is thinking of suicide, you should get an adult right away. It is too much responsibility for a kid. You can always call a hospital or mental health center or anyone you trust to be responsible. Waiting even a little time can make it *too late.*

Pay attention when someone says that she/he wants to commit suicide or if someone doesn't say it but looks lonely and withdrawn for a long time. It could help to talk to her/him. The most important thing is to give that person hope.

Remember that, as Amyee said, "It is easy to *say* sit down and talk about it. But if a person is determined to do it, it is often hard to sit down and think."

But if the person will talk, you should try to convince that person that it is wrong to do what he/she is going to do. As Darcey said, "Try to convince the person to wait one more day and see if the feelings are the same. There is always another day." Michelle said, "Kids need to know that the situation is never as bad as it seems." Things can always change when you get older.

Don't try to use "psychology" and tell them, "Good, kill yourself, I don't care," as a way to scare them out of it. It might work once or twice, but nobody ever knows when someone might commit suicide, even the experts.

Everybody thinks about committing suicide at one time or another; it is natural. There is nothing wrong with thinking about it, only with trying it.

VACATIONS: SINGLE-PARENT, STEPPARENT, TWO-PARENT

Single-parent:

My vacation was all right. My mom worked so I went over to my friend's house. I usually slept until about 10 A.M., which was good. I think if I had a two-parent family we would have gone on a vacation, like to Florida or something. That is really when I wish I had two parents who lived together!—Julie B.

My vacation was very boring! It wouldn't have made any difference if I had been living in a two-parent family. It would have been just as boring. My mother works so we wouldn't have been able to go anyplace anyway. If I had been in a two-parent family, they both would have been working, and I would have been just as bored.—Tina

My mother had to work so we spent time with my grandparents. We went out fishing but didn't catch anything. Also, I went to my friend's house. If I was in a two-parent family, I might have gone away, and I might have been able to spend more time with my mother. Probably, too, when I went shopping, instead of only getting two pairs of pants, I would have gotten a whole wardrobe because there would have been two paychecks instead of one.—Amyee

Stepparent:

My vacation wasn't affected by whether or not I was in a single-parent or a two-parent family. I stayed home all week. It was okay because I babysat and made thirty dollars. I wished that I had gone away, though.—Debby

It was just like any old vacation. I would ask my father if my girlfriend could come over, and he would say, "No." So I would ask my mother and she would say, "All right." If I was just living with my dad, she wouldn't have been able to come to the house.—Steve

Two-parent:

My vacation was okay. Mostly, I stayed home and watched my soap operas. On Friday, Saturday, and Sunday we went to Massachusetts and visited my sister. I went horseback riding and shopping. If I were in a single-parent family, I probably wouldn't have gone because my mom can't drive long distances, and my dad won't go anywhere far away without my mom.—Michelle

Friday, a friend asked me to go to Boston with her and her family. We had a lot of fun going to Quincy Market and the aquarium. I got back late Sunday and couldn't do much because of the snow. We were going to go to Pennsylvania to visit the Amish country, but it was storming there. I had a party Saturday and went to see the Outsiders. I went out to dinner Sunday with my mother and Dad and their friends. I was so bored that I almost fell asleep. Then yesterday, my mother grounded me for leaving things around the house and because I supposedly had a bad attitude. She would yell at me for having "that look" on my face, and I didn't have a "look." I can't really think of how my vacation would have been different if I had lived in a single-parent family, except maybe my mother wouldn't have been home to crab at me.—Margae

It was boring. If we had lived in a single-parent family, we might have gone out to dinner or to a movie.—Derek

6
Our Futures

We all think a lot about our futures and if they will be different because of having lived in single-parent families.

EVERYTHING CHANGES

Everything changes. Your family will change again, too. One parent may remarry or a boyfriend or girlfriend will move in. Maybe you will move in with the parent who is married and out of the single-parent household. Maybe the parent you live with will die. Your parents, after a long time, may even get remarried to each other! If none of those things happen, you will almost definitely eventually grow up and move out.

On Going into Stepfamilies

Families live as single-parent families for different periods of time—some for six months, some for two years, and some forever. The most common way that a single-parent family ends is for the single parent to remarry.

Kids usually find out from their parent that he/she is going to remarry. Michelle said, "It usually doesn't come as a big surprise. Most of the time the kids will know the person kind of well by the time a parent decides to remarry." That parent may break the news to them alone or with the person that he/she wants to marry. Sometimes a brother or sister overhears a conversation late at night between the parent and the person he/she wants to marry and tells the other kids. But, even if they aren't told and haven't overheard anything, Margae thought, "The kids just perceive that *something* is going to happen. They know inside that things are about to change."

We think that the decision whether or not to remarry is the parent's. Except in special cases where kids think that they may be in danger of abuse or of being very unhappy, kids shouldn't have the right to demand that a parent not marry the stepparent-to-be.

If you feel very strongly against the marriage, you should let it be known long before the marriage so that you can all talk about the feelings. Stephen said, "Also, if the stepparent-to-be treats you poorly, then you should bring that out." But kids shouldn't put undue pressure on their parents about the marriage. Margae said, "The parent should be able to marry whomever he or she wishes without feeling guilty."

We do think that kids should play some part in making the decision. Amyee said, "If the kids don't like the stepparent, they may be unhappy." Kids should know all that is going on and be able to voice their opinion. Depending on their ages, they should be able to decide if they want to live with the other parent instead of stay in the stepfamily.

Kids should tell their parents how they feel about the new stepparent. One girl said, "If you don't want to treat your stepparent like a mother figure or a father figure, you should talk to that person about how you feel and how you think you might handle the problem. It would work out a lot better if you sort out the problem instead of keeping your feelings inside. All my life, I kept my bad feelings about my stepparent inside. Just recently I got it out in the open, and I feel much better about it."

Families Can Prepare

Families can prepare to become stepfamilies before the marriage. How long it takes a family to adjust to being a stepfamily will depend on whether or not the kids want the change, on the expectations of the stepparent, and on the parent. Some families never adjust, but, as Noel said, "Many do well, and the kids appreciate their stepparent." We do think that the more effort people put into preparing, the less time the adjustment will take.

You could plan on some things not to change. Even after you get into the stepfamily, it doesn't always mean that you have to change the way you do things entirely. One girl said, "It can help if sometimes you do things without the stepparent. You don't always have to become a family."

The family should go through the change gradually, and kids should be kept *informed* because taking on a stepparent is scary. One girl said, "My mother started dating this guy. I didn't mind him. In fact, I kind of liked him. He was nice, and he liked my mother, my brother, and me. I just never thought of him as a father. When he and my mother got married, I just didn't understand anything. I think I didn't understand because I just wanted my father, the only father I ever knew." Tina said, "When parents remarry, a dream ends. To kids, remarriage of a parent can hurt because it means that there is now no chance of your parents getting back together."

There are a lot of things you miss when you go from a single-parent family to a stepfamily. Stephen said, "I think that the biggest thing a kid misses is the attention from the single parent." Having your mom or your dad there for just you can feel great. Roger said, "I was really jealous when my mother remarried. I would give her a hard time, be a brat, and fight with my sister all the time." You just get used to the closeness and the special relationship with your parent. A lot of times kids lose some of the freedom that they have grown used to as well. Michelle said, "I think kids would miss the privacy and the independence."

The new stepparent (and his/her children, if there are any) should be around your family a lot before the change becomes permanent. Jenny said, "The family could spend more time together and get all their feelings out in the open and not keep offending thoughts in." Darcey said, "Parents and kids should sit down with the person coming into the family and talk over new rules." It is hard for kids to accept someone other than their parent having the right to discipline them. Derek thought it would be a good idea for "the kids to be able to spend maybe a week with just the new stepparent to get to know that person better and to see what would happen."

A lot of times kids and stepparents start out as enemies. As Jenny said, "Kids can get so attached to the lost parent that they never give the stepparent a chance." One girl said, "It isn't that you really hate the stepparent, it's just that you feel that you can never replace your real parent." As Derek said, "Kids feel that the other parent still loves them no matter what happened." Sometimes, too, kids stay back from a stepparent because of the fear that this new person might leave or die like the other parent.

The good thing is that often, if everyone tries, they grow into getting along. Michelle said, "If a kid doesn't have a mother or father for a long time (like when a parent dies or leaves), that kid is more likely to take on a stepparent as a parent." Margae said, "The movie *On Golden Pond* showed how this can happen. At first, the boy in the movie hated the grandfather, who was a kind of stepparent, but after a while they loved each other."

Deciding what to call a stepparent can be hard. Some kids like to call a stepparent by the person's first name. It can take a while to get comfortable about calling somebody "Dad" or "Mom." Often this hurts the stepparent's feelings or makes your parent sad. The important thing is to talk about it so that everyone understands what you are feeling.

It Can Be Good

We all have ideas of ideal stepparents, and they are all different. One boy said, "I would want someone who cares about me and how I feel and loves me. Somebody who would take me to ball games and things like that." Some of us would like a person with a good sense of humor who is fun to be around. The most important thing, though, is that the person would be loving and caring to our parent (and also give in to our side once in a while).

We think that there are benefits for kids in changing from a single-parent family to a stepfamily if the change is wanted by everyone. It can be a new experience for the whole family in which everyone learns to deal with new life situations. Amyee said, "For one thing, it is like having a spare tire for your car. The stepparent can be there when you need someone." Darcey said, "There is often more money in stepfamilies and less household duties for kids. Your parent seems happier, too, because he or she has a companion." If the stepparent has kids and you can get along, it is like having a new family.

STAYING A SINGLE-PARENT FAMILY

Many kids now live in single-parent families throughout their lives. More and more parents are choosing to stay single. Some parents enjoy the independent living. They are happy and don't want to have to cope with the compromises that go along with living with a spouse. Tom said, "Parents might want to keep the freedoms to do what they want, like date, and not get weighed down by a spouse."

Some parents aren't interested in marriage but just enjoy being a parent. For them, as Noel said, "Raising a child is enough." They may want to prove to themselves that they can handle the responsibilities and raise the kids the way they want. Other parents may still be afraid of losing someone or having a marriage fail again.

For many kids, this is fine. Change is hard. Most kids remember the havoc of getting into a single-parent family. They are always somewhat afraid of getting hurt again. And there are a number of kids who like the family and don't want it to change again. Amyee said, "You get settled down and used to being in a single-parent family and don't want to face the possibility of another divorce." After you make one big change and finally get comfortable, Noel said, "you think that if the family changes again everything is going to get totally messed up."

Worries of Losing Your Parent

One thing about living with a single parent is the fear that your parent will die and leave you with no parent. Amyee said, "Once my mother got into an accident, and now I always feel like she is going to get into another one and die."

You get afraid that there is nobody else for you and that you will have to go to a foster home or live out on the streets. Some kids fear that they will have to live with a parent they are now quite distant from.

Some kids don't think about it because, as Sheri said, "They don't want to!" Other kids accept it as a possibility. Tom said, "I try to be an optimist about the future. When it comes to death, though, I am a fatalist. If it happens, it happens. I might not like it, *but there is nothing that I can do about it.*" But we think that most kids wonder, as Missy does: "My mom is the only parent who I have left, and I love her. I have always wondered what I would do without her if she died."

We think kids and parents should have plans for the possibility of something awful happening to their single parent. It is also important to feel you can talk about death freely. Sheri said, "You should know who you would be able to live with."

A lot of families have talked about it. One girl said, "After my father died, my mother put it in her will that if something happened to her, we would go live with my uncle." Michelle said, "My sister set it up so that each of the kids has a place to go and that they will get a certain amount of money to pay for their expenses. At eighteen, they can do what they choose."

Leaving Home

All kids are afraid of growing up and leaving home. They are afraid of drugs and alcohol, of peer pressure, of not being able to handle a serious relationship, and of making decisions. As Margae said, "You can't be sure that your decisions are right until you are looking back on them." Every kid wants to grow up to be something and to be wanted by someone.

For some kids, leaving home from a single-parent family will not be as hard as from a two-parent family. Elizabeth said, "There will be only one parent to leave and not two. Also, some kids have grown independent long before it is time to leave home."

For a lot of us, it will be more difficult. You have grown so close to your parent and your parent to you. You may have a hard time convincing your parent that it is all right for you to move out. Tom said, "I think that kids in single-parent families get closer to their parents than kids in two-parent families seem to."

Amyee said, "You will worry about your parent being left alone." Julie B. said, "I think the one thing that is going to bother me is the guilt of leaving my mother by herself because she has done so much for me." You worry a lot about your parent being very lonely, especially if you are the last child. This is why the older you become the more you can tolerate the idea of your parent remarrying and hope he/she can find someone to share life with. It helps you to feel better about leaving home.

Kids have their own fears about leaving, too. You wonder, "Will I make it? Will I turn out like my parents? Will I be a success?" It is scary to leave the parent you love. You are afraid that you will become a single parent, even if you don't want to, and that you might not have enough money to support your child or children.

We do think that kids will be more cautious about going into relationships when they grow up and will try harder when they do get involved. One girl said, "I'm bitter. I have a hurt inside that I refuse to give up. I will always be a little leery of relationships." Amyee said, "I am not going to rush into anything." It is important to kids not to make the same mistakes that their parents made. Missy said, "You might not trust as easily as if you had been raised in a two-parent family with no divorce or death."

We think that some kids will be afraid to get married and have children at all. You feel as cautious about having children as you do about getting married. You won't want a child of yours to have to go through what you have gone through. Or you worry, as Tina said, "because you only know the experience of living with one parent. If you get married and have children, you might try to take on all the responsibility."

Kids should know that:

Just because your parents made mistakes, you don't have to make the same ones. Divorce isn't hereditary.

Take your time. Pick someone who interests you and try not to be afraid to show your feelings.

Be confident. You will be able to handle it. Tell yourself that your parents' problems aren't your problems. If you go into a relationship with a bad attitude, you might create the problems you fear.

Be patient with the person you choose.

Don't settle for less than you deserve.

It is important to remember that, as Ms. Sweeney said, "Kids don't necessarily do the same as their parents. I think that people's experience of a family is partly the family they are in but also the other kinds of families they are exposed to. Most people are able to choose what they want."

When We Are Adults

Our fantasies of the future are just the same as anybody's: gorgeous spouse, beautiful kids, big house, nice car, good relationships, rich and happy.

We think that growing up in single-parent families does affect your expectations of the future. For one thing, you always want to know what a two-parent family is like. For another, you are more realistic. You take life more seriously. You know that bad things like divorce or death can happen. We think this will make us, as Noel said, "push harder" to get the things we want.

We think, too, that kids who grow up in single-parent families know a lot about family relations. It makes you stronger and more likely to have your own opinions about your family and more willing to stand your own ground. This could make it hard to have a relationship with someone who doesn't know as much about families as you do.

We think that we will always remain closer to the parent we lived with, even after we grow up. Elizabeth said, "I will always be close to my mom and protective of her. My dad and I will probably always get along." We think that you just understand that parent better and realize how hard it was to raise you alone. In a way, you will always want to pay them back. Noel said, "When I grow up, I think that I might understand everything that she had to go through with me."

Most of us have images of being there for our parents and supporting the decisions that they make for themselves. We picture making a lot of money so that our parents don't have to work so hard and can buy anything they might want. One girl said, "If my parent ever needs money or moral support, I will be there for her just like she was for me. I think that she deserves at least that."

GIVING UP THE ANGER

We doubt that you ever completely stop thinking about things that happen to you. Joan Goodrich, a single parent we interviewed, said, "Children have a lot of feelings, and you have to deal with them from the time of the divorce—forever. I don't think those feelings ever go away. We still talk about them. It is not as difficult as it was when I was just divorced, but there are still issues that come up. I thought I could get them to understand by explaining it to them and 'working it out.' I thought I could talk them out of their feelings, but you can't do that." We think that it's the same if a parent dies.

Giving up the anger can be hard. One girl said, "I can't give it up. It keeps me going. When you stay angry, it keeps you from feeling that a parent left because of you. You believe that your parent left because of his or her own problems." Most kids think that when things happen it has to be somebody's fault.

It will take a while to come to the realization that what has happened in your life is no one's fault—not yours, not your parent's, not anyone's. When you finally accept it, you can start to let go of the anger. Talking to people (parents or friends) or writing feelings down can help. Writing, in particular, can be a great release for emotions. Also, it gives you a chance to go back and read what you have said and maybe make some discoveries about yourself.

Learning not to hate, not to dwell on the past, not to think "What if?" or "Why didn't I?" and to forgive and let go is a long slow process. But it is certainly possible; anything is.

Book Reviews

***** Excellent
**** Pretty Good
*** Satisfactory
** Fair
* Terrible

My Mother Is Not Married to My Father, by Jean Davies Okimoto (published by G. P. Putnam's Sons, 1979)

Julie Haynes reviewed this book and rated it ****.

Summary: This book is about a girl named Cynthia Browne. She and her sister are going through the torment of their parents getting a divorce. After the divorce, they have to get used to their father dating and then their mother dating. They have different feelings, such as hatred and confusion. They also go through being in joint custody, which brings up most of the confusion. Toward the end of the book, the confusion of Cynthia's family situation causes her to give up the lead in her school play. Later on her feelings are put back together when her mother becomes engaged to a man both Cynthia and her little sister, Sara, approve of highly.

Comment: I think that this book could help kids with parental dating and remarriage. It wouldn't help kids in long-term single-parent families because Cynthia was only in one for a short time. The dating part is like my own experiences when I assumed my parent was going to get married right away.

Confessions of a Teenage Baboon, by Paul Zindel (published by Harper & Row, 1977)

Stephen Peters reviewed this book and rated it ***.

Summary: This book is about a kid named Chris. He lives on Staten Island, New York. When Chris was five, his father went to get the evening paper and never came back. The dude has been gone for almost ten years. (Talk about taking your time!)

Chris has a so-called friend, Lloyd Dipardi. Chris's mother is taking care of Lloyd's dying mother. One day Lloyd tells Chris off. He says things like "You're retarded" and "Some kids are taught how to take care of themselves, but you've missed the boat." That makes Chris feel bad. But then Lloyd teaches Chris to stand up for what he is.

Comment: Nobody can tell you who to be. You have to figure it out for yourself. I think Chris was scared of his feelings and didn't understand why his father left. Eventually, he does understand and gets used to it. He gets more independent because of it and doesn't rely on what everybody else thinks—just his own feelings.

Father Figure, by Richard Peck (published by Viking Press, 1978)

Elizabeth Albrycht reviewed this book and rated it ***.

Summary: Jim Atwater's mother commits suicide. Jim's father, who left them eight years ago, shows up at the funeral. Jim, his brother, and their father don't have much to say. After the funeral, their father goes back to Florida. A month or two later, Jim's brother is mugged and his collarbone is broken. His father comes to visit again. After he leaves, Jim's grandmother sends Jim and his brother to Florida for the summer to live with their dad. Jim and his father get off to a bad start. Jim resents him for leaving his mother. Eventually, Jim and his father have a truce.

Comment: Jim is angry and bitter about having a father who has never been around. He is also jealous of his brother's new relationship with their father. This book shows the effort and growing up both Jim and his father had to do.

Domestic Arrangements, by Norma Klein (published by M. Evans, 1981)

Tina Carey reviewed this book and rated it ****.

Summary: During this story a girl's father has to go away, and one night she notices that another man is with her mother. She isn't quite sure if her mother is having an affair or not so she keeps quiet. Then, she finds out her father may also be having an affair. After a while, her parents realize they are in love with other people and decide on a divorce. She isn't really upset because of her suspicions in the first place, but she is a little hurt because she loves both of her parents very much.

Comment: This book isn't really about a divorce but about what leads up to a divorce. This situation is like mine because my parents separated and divorced in a similar way.

I, Trissy, by Norma Fox Mazer (published by Delacorte Press, 1971)

Amyee Robinson reviewed this book and rated it ***.

Summary: Trissy Beer's parents get separated. When she finds out that her father is seeing another woman, she burns everything he ever gave to her. Then, to make it worse, she and her best friend get into a fight. When Trissy goes out to a boat exhibit, she gets lost and has to walk fifty-seven blocks back to her house. She is always getting punished for things she does. At the end, she and her best friend get back together and she accepts her father. Then, her mother gets married, and Trissy is really happy.

Comment: I think that this book could help kids know how to cope and face the fact that their parents can date.

Gardine vs. *Hanover,* by Joan L. Oppenheimer (published by Thomas Y. Crowell, 1982)

Sheri Mulready reviewed this book and rated it *****.

Summary: This book is about a girl named Jill. Jill's mom gets married, and Jill hates her new stepsister. They are always fighting. Then, her mom and stepfather separate because of the kids. Everyone is miserable after the separation. Jill thought it would be better, but it isn't. Jill's sister, Abby, won't talk to her, and her mom is always so sad. Jill misses her stepfather, too, but she still thinks that it is Caroline's fault.

Finally, both girls come to their senses and talk. Jill and Caroline realize that they broke their parents up, and they have to get their parents back together. This time they don't have to be a family; they want to be a family.

Comment: Reading about Jill's family could help kids understand what a strain they can cause on a new marriage. This book has a happy ending. Sometimes things don't end up this happy.

Out of Love, by Hilma Wolitzer (published by Farrar, Straus & Giroux, 1978)

Julie Bird reviewed this book and rated it **.

Summary: Teddy Hecht is a very confused girl. Her parents are divorced. She reads all of her parents' old love letters and doesn't understand how they could fall in love and out of love so fast. She tries to find answers, but school and quizzes in teen magazines don't help. Teddy's younger sister, Karen, doesn't seem curious or even mad about it. Instead, she puts on an act that Teddy also can't understand. One day, she and her best friend are in the same situation, and they decide to make up their minds to live with it because nothing is going to change. Well, it does change. She and her friend talk about it every day, and after a while they become normal again.

Comment: I think this book would be good for kids to help cope with and under-stand about their parents' divorce. It also helps you open up and express your feelings.

Chloris and the Weirdos, by Kin Platt (published by Bradbury Press, 1978)

Tom Haley reviewed this book and rated it *****.

Summary: This story is about Jenny's and her sister's experiences with their mother and her boyfriends. Jenny's boyfriend, Harold, is a skateboard freak whose mother is also divorced. He gives a lot of good advice to Jenny on how to handle her mother and her sister. Finally, her sister and her mom get into a fight, and her sister runs away.

Comment: This story gives a lot of advice on what to do in different situations. It stresses talking things out. It doesn't go too far into one subject so you don't get bored.

Sometimes I Think I Hear My Name, by Avi (published by Pantheon Books, 1982)

Julie Haynes reviewed this book and rated it *.

Summary: This book, to put it plainly, isn't good. It is about a boy whose parents are divorced. He lives with his aunt and uncle. The boy is supposed to go to England on vacation, but he decides to run away. When he gets to his mother's house, he finds out that she doesn't want him. When he gets to his father's house, he discovers that his father doesn't really want him either. Heartbroken, he has to go back to his other relatives.

Comment: This book is awful. It is short, stupid, and unconvincing. If the boy had really wanted to be with his parents, he would have tried harder. Another thing, there isn't much emotion in the book. Conrad doesn't cry or anything when he finds out that his parents don't want him.

None of the Above, by Rosemary Wells (published by the Dial Press, 1974)

Margae Diamond reviewed this book and rated it *.

Summary: This is a story about Marcia Mill, a senior in high school. She and her sister are forced to live with their stepmother and her two kids when Marcia's dad remarries. She hates her stepmother and falls into a bad rut at school. Her marks are very low, and she spends her free time shopping and drinking soda with her friend. When she is at home, she fights with her stepmother and stepsister and watches television all the time. Marcia has a bad time adjusting to a new environ-ment, and she just gives up trying to be what her parents would like her to be.

Comment: I don't think this book would help a kid because it has no thoughts or ideas on how to come out of a situation like this one. It has a really negative attitude. Nothing good happens to this girl. It would make the kid reading this story feel like giving up.

Getting Nowhere, by Constance C. Greene (published by the Viking Press, 1977)

Derek Hurley reviewed this book and rated it ****.

Summary: This book is about a boy whose father gets remarried. The boy doesn't like his stepmother in the beginning. In the middle, Mark (the boy) starts to like her, and by the end they become good friends.

Comment: This tells about ways for kids to cope with a stepmother. The most important thing is that it shows the new parent is not responsible for what happened to the other parent.

My Other-Mother, My Other-Father, by Harriet Langsam Sobol (published by Macmillan, 1979)

Faith Tudor reviewed this book and rated it **.

Summary: Andrea talks to her teacher, Mrs. Burns, all the time. Some of the things she talks about are her family and school. Andrea's family is very complicated. Her mother is remarried to a man whose name is Larry Goodrich. She still remembers when she had to call him Mr. Goodrich, but now she calls him Larry. Andrea has trouble in school explaining her family. She gets embarrassed when friends ask her why her name is different from her mother's. Andrea's father is remarried, too. Andrea has a very complicated life.

Comment: I would not recommend this book for older kids because there wasn't enough detail in it. It didn't tell you about her family and her personal feelings. There weren't any examples to explain her different experiences. Younger kids might like it.

It's Not the End of the World, by Judy Blume (published by Bradbury Press, 1972)

Michelle Burrington reviewed and rated this book ****.

Summary: In the beginning, Karen's parents fight all the time. Karen thinks they are just going through a stage, but one night her father storms out of the house and never comes back. Her little sister, Amy, is very upset. Her brother becomes very withdrawn, and Karen can't talk to anyone. Then one day her brother runs away. She hopes her parents will get back together because of her brother, but they don't. After her brother comes back, her mom goes back to school, and Karen, Jeff, and Amy learn to take care of themselves. They visit their father a lot after the divorce, and they all realize divorce isn't the end of the world.

Comment: This book teaches kids that divorce doesn't have to mean the end of everything good in a kid's life. It would be better, though, if it explained what a divorce was more fully.

Tiger Eyes by Judy Blume (published by Bradbury Press, 1981)

Margae Diamond reviewed this book and rated it *****.

Summary: This book covers going into a single-parent family by death. It takes you through the girl's experience, her reactions to her mom, a new home, death, and the people around her.

Comment: It is EXCELLENT.

Paul Dolmetsch, M.S.W., is a psychiatric social worker with United Counseling Service of Bennington County, Vermont. Paul grew up the youngest of four children in a single-parent family. He attended the University of Delaware and received his B.A. in psychology in 1974. Following completion of his undergraduate degree, he served as a VISTA Volunteer in East Texas where he developed and directed programs for youth. In 1976 he entered the University of Texas at Austin School of Social Work and completed a M.S.W. degree. Since that time, he has specialized in services for adolescents and their families. These services include individual and family therapy, consultation to schools and social service systems, public speaking and parent education programs, and innovative techniques to tap adolescent creativity. Mr. Dolmetsch has been married to Gail Mauricette for twelve years and has two children, Stephanie and Jason.

Alexa Shih is a marketing specialist in programs for adolescents. Born in 1944, she was graduated from Pennsylvania State University with a B.A. in English. She began her career as an editorial researcher for *Reader's Digest* and as a freelance writer. She is currently on staff at United Counseling Service of Bennington County, Vermont, and regularly provides consultation to parent groups and schools interested in single-parent issues. Ms. Shih has been a single parent for seven years and lives with her three children, Peter, Polly, and Isobel.